High Wycombe's Contribution to Aviation

A history of events and those involved from the earliest days of flight.

Researched and written by David Scott and Ian Simmons

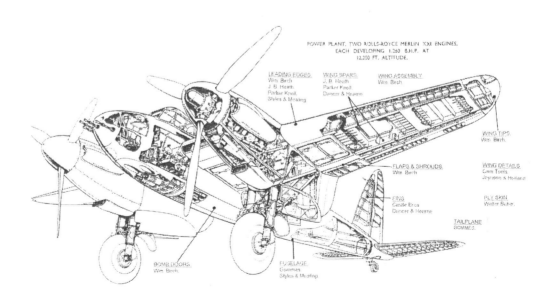

DEDICATION

This book is dedicated to the craftsmen and women of this town's furniture industry, who during both World Wars played such an important part in the production of two unique aircraft. At that time they were the most advanced of their type in the world. During the First World War it was parts for the D.H.4 day bomber that they produced, an aircraft that proved to be faster than most fighter aircraft of the day. In the Second World War the D.H.98 Mosquito repeated this same attribute and for over two years remained the fastest aircraft in the world. Both aircraft carried the D.H. initials. The origin of those initials was a man born locally and considered one of the most versatile of those early pioneers within the British aircraft industry, Geoffrey de Havilland.

In the furniture industry, for those craftsmen and craftswomen involved on aircraft work, the standard of workmanship was the highest ever achieved, equalling that of true engineering. At the industry's better times it employed more than 70% of the town's workforce.

Unfortunately today most of the firms involved, some very small, others that became household names in the production of fine furniture, are no longer with us. Yet for many years they were the backbone of our town's industry and its prosperity. They had earned a reputation for production of fine furniture second to none. Workers in the industry during the war years had shown an ability far in advance of anything they had done before or since and in doing so earned the respect of all who designed and flew those outstanding aircraft.

High Wycombe was for so many years universally known and respected simply and honestly as,
"The Furniture Town."

Sadly today little remains of our once flourishing industry.

Ian C. Simmons
March 2007

ISBN 978-0-9558241-1-1

© 2008 David Scott & Ian Simmons.

Published by David Scott & Ian Simmons.
154 New Road, Booker, High Wycombe,
Bucks. HP12 4LA.

First published 2007 by Wycombe District Council.
This revised edition, 2008.

Printed by Wycombe District Council.

b

FOREWORD
By Christopher Woodman

The age of powered human flight began just over a century ago. But High Wycombe's aviation history may be said to have begun in 1882 with the birth of the great Sir Geoffrey de Havilland, whose famous "DH" initials were to grace aircraft from the DH1 reconnaissance biplane of 1915 through to the DH106 Comet airliner and the DH125 business jets which are still in service with the Royal Air Force today.

Almost from the beginning of the aeroplane era, High Wycombe witnessed the unfolding of aviation history. Later it was to play a vital part in the development of the aircraft industry and in supplying aircraft that helped win two World Wars.

In 1911 Mr Henry Astley landed a version of the Bleriot XI monoplane at Saunderton, and in 1912 the legendary Col. Cody came to Downley.

With the outbreak of the First World War, Wycombe's furniture factories became heavily involved in the war effort, building aircraft wings and parts, although many skilled workers were redeployed to aircraft factories elsewhere in Southern England. Eventually all the great names of Wycombe furniture manufacturers banded together to build the town's own aircraft factory in Hughenden Avenue, but no sooner was this completed than the War came to an end, and aircraft production with it.

After 1918 came the "barnstorming years". Many young Wycombe people had their first taste of flight when Alan Cobham's Flying Circus came to town in 1932-35. It is from that time that we see fabulous aerial photographs of our town in transition, with today's roads built, but not yet with their full complement of houses. In those days, aircraft landed at Whincup's field at the top of Marlow Hill – it was not until 1939 that an aerodrome was licensed at Booker.

By the time the Second World War broke out, most aircraft were built of metal – but not all. The splendid exception was the DH Mosquito – made of wood and faster than a Spitfire. Dancer & Hearne, Styles & Mealing and William Birch were among the firms who built wings and fuselages for these wonderful aircraft. In the High Street, Davenport Vernon, whose skills were in metal, refurbished Wellington bomber fuselages. Out of town, Hughenden Manor was code-named "Hillside" – a secret so well-kept that not until the 1980s did it emerge that this had been a top map-making facility throughout World War II.

And so to the present era, of RAF Strike Command, RAF Daws Hill (soon to be filled with desirable new homes) and Wycombe Air Park. Many – but not all – of the furniture factories are gone. The roads on Cressex Business Park bear testimony to the bombers such as the Halifax, Stirling and Lancaster, parts for which were made there. The memory of Sir Geoffrey de Havilland is celebrated in the naming of De Havilland Drive in Terriers and a green plaque on Terriers House.

It is all a gripping story, engrossingly told by David Scott and Ian Simmons. We owe them a great debt for the work they have done to bring together so many details of a distinctive part of our town's long history.

NOTES ON SOURCE MATERIAL AND ACKNOWLEDGEMENTS

Our especial thanks to Stuart McKay MBE Secretary of the DH Moth Club, for his help and reading our draft manuscript and suggesting corrections and amendments as necessary, also to Christopher Woodman for his final reading.

To all those who have given so willingly, their time, information, help, photographs and other material used to compile this record of local aviation interest, for their encouragement during this endeavour, we the compilers, Dave Scott and Ian Simmons both extend our thanks.

Barry Guess, Mike Fielding and Ron Hedges (BAE Heritage), Joanna Tiddy (Wycombe District Council Heritage Officer), Mike Bomford, Stella Eglinton and Fiona Chandler (Wycombe District Council), James Rattue, Madalyn Green, Catherine Grigg & staff (Wycombe Museum), James Everett (Aylesbury County Museum), Mrs. F.E.Valiant (Wycombe Abbey School), Gerry Tyack (Wellington Museum, Morton-in-Marsh), Ken Hyde (Shuttleworth Collection), Anne Essex (née de Havilland), Charles Batkin and John Stride (de Havilland Heritage Centre), Tim Lewis (RAF Strike Command), Pat Bramley (Bucks Free Press), Colin Cruddas (Cobham and BHAP), Eric Heath (Heathfield Furniture), Richard Hearne, A.A.Smith, Norman Stanners and Ron Johnston (Dancer & Hearne), Andrew Mealing (Styles & Mealing), Bill Davis (Davis & Davis), Frank Glenister (Glenisters), David Gomme, Bob Warne and Mrs. Dumbleton (E. Gomme Ltd.), John Broom-Smith (Broom & Wade), Jessie Binns, Ros Lee and Mary Edwards (National Trust, Hughenden Manor), Mrs. Oliver wife of the late Andrew Oliver (Walter Baker), Albert Ivermee (Walter Baker), Mr. D. Langston (Davenport Vernon), Norman Belson and Doreen Biggins (Downley and Cody), Graham Twitchen, Dr. Rachel Brown and Roberta Wilson (Booker Airfield), Lewis Perrin (Booker Airfield photos), Mike Osborne (Airfield Research Group, Air Britain), Malcolm Fillmore and Barry Abraham (Air Britain), John Lunnon (Doolittle article), Nick Welland-Robinson (North Dean), Andrew Abbott (Timber Research Association), Justin Fowler (Bourne End), Brian Print and Ken Townsend (Bourne End Flying Field), Ron Setter, Peter and Pearl Halliday (Chiltern Aircraft Research Group), Alec Astrop (Ministry of Aircraft Production), Tony Pearce, (Mr. W.G.Chapman article), Bob Hickox and Don Tilbury (Lacey Green), Bob and Olive Mead (Styles & Mealing Pictures), Dave Briggs (WW2 Aerial Pictures), Mr and Mrs. Hearne (Plastalune), John Hanham (Princes Risborough), Peter Harris (West Wycombe WW1), Tony Bianchi (Personal Plane Services), Mr. and Mrs. West (Stocken Farm, Lacey Green Airstrip), Ivan Sparkes, Anthony Emery, John Gray, Victor Collins and the late Donald Hill. (And also Maureen Simmons whose patience and cups of tea have kept us going.)

Our apologies to all who have contributed and are not mentioned through our failing memories.

References used

Bucks Free Press. BAE Systems Archives. Wycombe Museum. Wycombe Abbey School. "A Chiltern Village School" (Joan West). "Hallmark, The Lacey Green and Loosley Row Magazine." "A Celebration of 130 Years of Service" (History of Davenport Vernon). "A Furniture Maker" (Lucian R. Ercolani). "High Wycombe, England's Furniture Town," High Wycombe Furniture Manufacturing Society. "The History of Chair Making in High Wycombe" (Mayes). "Wycombe Chair-makers in Camera" (Ivan Sparkes), "High Wycombe Heritage Trail" (Wycombe District Council). Public Records Office, Shuttleworth Collection Archive Library. de Havilland Heritage Centre. "The Aeroplane Directory" 1952. General Register Office. Dictionary of National Biography. Aylesbury County Archives. Kelly's Directories. "The Cabinet Maker and Complete House Furnisher." "Cabinet Maker and Retail Furnisher" (September 1980). "Wood", (September and November 1945). "Take a Seat, The Story of Parker Knoll 1834–1994," (Stephen Bland). "A Recorded History of CompAir / Broom & Wade" (H.S.Broom). Science Museum. Air Britain. "Flying" (July 1933). "Sky Fever, The Autobiography of Sir Geoffrey de Havilland" (Airlife Publishing 1979). "The de Havilland Aircraft Company" (Maurice Allward and John Taylor). Images of Aviation (Tempus Publishing, 1996). "DH. An Outline of de Havilland History" (Martin Sharp). "Construction of the DH 98 Mosquito" (A de Havilland Heritage Centre Publication, reprinted from "Aircraft Production" June 1943). "Mosquito" (Martin Sharp and Michael Bowyer). "The Mosquito Log" (Alexander McKee). "The Mosquito Manual" (Arms and Armour, RAF Museum). "The Mosquito 50 Years on" (Royal Aeronautical Society Symposium, 1990). "Mosquito. The Illustrated History" (Philip J.Birtles, Sutton Publishing 1999). "Mosquito. Wooden Wonder" (Edward Bishop, Pan/Ballantine 1971). "Flight". "Aeroplane". "The Aeroplane" (September 4 1953). "Aeronautics." "Flypast." "More Tails of the Fifties" (Peter G. Campbell, Cirrus Associates). "In Cobham's Company. Sixty Years of Flight Refuelling Limited" (Colin Cruddas, Cobham plc 1994). "Cobham. The Flying Years" (Colin Cruddas, Archive Photograph Series, The Chalford Publishing Company. 1997). "Those Fabulous Flying Years" (Colin Cruddas, Air Britain 2003). "Rotol, The History of an Airscrew Company, 1937–1960" (Bruce Stait, Alan Sutton Publishing 1990). "Airco" (Mick Davis, Crowood Press 2001). "Wings over Woodley. The Story of Miles Aircraft and the Adwest Group" (Julian C. Temple, Aston Publications). "After the Battle" Issue 87 ("The High Wycombe Air Headquarters, Royal Air Force and U.S. Eighth Army Air Force", Battle of Britain Prints International Ltd.). British Library (Newspaper Division). "Chiltern Prangs" (Ron Setter, Peter and Pearl Halliday).

CONTENTS

Dedication

Foreword by Christopher Woodman

Acknowledgements

CHAPTER 1

PRE - 1914. THE EARLY PIONEERING YEARS

There is a flight recorded on 12th November 1784, by a balloonist James Sadler, who on his second attempt flew from an unknown point in Oxfordshire and landed near Aylesbury, having apparently travelled a distance of fourteen miles. The famous Montgolfier brothers had made their first balloon ascent on 4th June 1783. Experiments with early gliders gave some experience in controlling these early airborne contraptions. The first theories of flight had begun to be tested. In fact flight had been achieved long before the Wright brothers' first successful attempt at "powered" flight, yet there can be no denying theirs was the first step in the development of true aviation, as we understand it today.

Aviation's pioneering years, from the Wrights' first powered flight in America on 17th December 1903 until the outbreak of the First World War, were probably, for those involved, the most dangerous in its history. A few brave men of vision began to embrace this new enterprise. At first, with no one to teach them the rudiments of flying, all they could do was cautiously try their new ideas. The fortunate ones managed to reap benefits from their efforts, some were destined to become leaders in this newly emerging industry, but many failed. More than a hundred years have now passed since the first of those early endeavours into powered flight. We now know their efforts were worthwhile, yet then they had no idea of the enormity of what they had started.

Looking back, we find several aviation events in the High Wycombe area that were, thankfully, carefully reported in the local newspapers. Maybe not earth-shattering events, but interesting, as well as deserving to be remembered as a part of our local aviation history. Such events help to broaden our understanding as we have the benefit of still knowing intimately the area in which they took place.

One such event was the landing made by Col. Samuel Franklin Cody at Downley in 1912, which drew people from all around Wycombe to see his aeroplane. For many in the town, this was their first chance to see one of these strange contraptions at close quarters. Strange contraptions they were then, simply because they were something new, but as we look at them today, perhaps they look even stranger as we can compare them to our modern aircraft. How crude they seem now!

George Holt Thomas, a local resident, was among those deeply involved in the newly emerging industry. His father, William Thomas, was founder of the Daily Graphic newspaper in London. Holt Thomas, as he was more usually known, resided for a time in Wooburn Green and later in North Dean. In 1912 he founded the Aircraft Manufacturing Company (A.M.C.), later known as Airco, at Hendon. He started by building, under licence, the French 'Farman' aircraft. Three of these took part in an event reported in the Bucks Free Press of the time as "The Battle of Booker", a wide-ranging army manoeuvre held in 1913. The Army Flying Corps used these aircraft at the start of the First World War. High Wycombe's furniture industry's significant involvement with aircraft production during the war was mainly due to his influence.

On the outskirts of High Wycombe another event preceded some of these (though not recognised as an event of any importance at the time). On 27th July 1882, Alice, wife of Rev. Charles de Havilland, then a curate at Holy Trinity Church at Hazlemere, gave birth to their second son. He was named Geoffrey and was destined to become one of the most versatile and prolific pioneers within the British aircraft industry, eventually being rewarded with a knighthood for his services to aviation. He too had a great impact on Wycombe's furniture industry during both World Wars. Strangely, with the passing of time, all evidence of his birthplace had become lost. Even his family had no idea of the location. In his autobiography, *'Sky Fever'*, it is simply passed over as a village near High Wycombe. Happily today this mystery has been resolved.

SEARCHING FOR THE BIRTHPLACE OF SIR GEOFFREY DE HAVILLAND

During a visit in the summer of 1998 to the Shuttleworth Aircraft Collection at Old Warden, Bedfordshire, Dave Scott, co-author of this book and a long-standing aircraft enthusiast, found something he could not understand. At the entrance to one of the exhibition buildings usually referred to as the 'de Havilland' hangar he paused to read the information board provided by the Moth Club. It referred to "Sir Geoffrey, - born in a village near High Wycombe".

As this was where Dave was living, he became curious as to the precise location. Enquiries were made to the Shuttleworth Trust, Stuart McKay of the de Havilland Moth Club, then Philip Birtles at the de Havilland Heritage Museum. None of them were able to give a positive answer, although Philip Birtles thought it to be Wooburn, a village to the east of High Wycombe, but knew no more. Reference to the 1881 Census proved a de Havilland family had certainly lived there, but only Ivon, Geoffrey's elder brother, had been born there in 1879. By the following census of 1891, there was no further evidence of the family being there.

An inquiry to Robert Thompson, then of the Genealogy Society, provided a copy of Sir Geoffrey's birth certificate. This gave positive proof of the birthplace being - Magdala House, Terriers, on the 27th July 1882. With this information it would be relatively simple to locate the property. Unfortunately it was not so – a property of this name could not be found around the Terriers area. So what had happened to Magdala House? Had it been demolished? Surely somehow, somewhere the site must be known. At that time it seemed the search had come to a dead end again, yet Anne Essex (née de Havilland), Sir Geoffrey's granddaughter, encouraged Dave to continue. She had heard about the search, via the Moth Club, and had understandably become interested.

Seeking further information in local books, Dave was fortunate to find a book on Hazlemere, written by David Gantzel. There were several references to the Reverend Charles de Havilland's family, showing that the family, the Reverend Charles, his wife Alice and son Ivon, lived there from 1880 to 1883, while Charles was curate at Holy Trinity Church, Hazlemere. As it was during this time that their second son Geoffrey had been born (1882), could any further evidence be found in older maps of the area? Unfortunately none was found that gave any indication of the house names in the area.

Wycombe District Council's Heritage Officer, Joanna (Jo.) Tiddy, now willingly joined the hunt.

Dave provided her with all the evidence he had collected to date. From this it seemed to indicate that a property today known as "Flint Cottage" might be the former Magdala House, but this was by no means conclusive. By the early summer of 1999, after making some door to door enquiries, Dave felt the property now known as Terriers Green House was the more likely answer. The census of 1881 had shown that the Rev. de Havilland had three live-in servants, which must indicate a larger house than "Flint Cottage." He called on the owner, a Mr. Alan Oldham, who was convinced there could be no connection.

Further research included reference to Ordnance Survey maps of the period, the Royal Mail Archives, the Land Register, the Holy Trinity Church records in the County Records Office at Aylesbury and appeals in the local press. This was followed up by contact with some of the older local residents. All this was to no avail. Further investigation conducted by Jo Tiddy in the County Record Office found an unedited version of a narrative from David Gantzel's book. With this was a handwritten account by a Mrs. J. Putnam, and it listed the residences passed whilst walking along the road from the Turnpike Gate at Terriers on towards Hazlemere, these corresponding exactly to the census data. Of crucial importance though, in the unedited version were the words, *"Reverend de Havilland - on the green"*.

Terriers Green House would have been, as it still is, the sole property *"on the green"*. All other residences mentioned at this point were on the other side of the road. Unfortunately no records in the public domain gave any indication as to who may have rented the house, or its previous name(s). Jo was also now convinced that Terriers Green House must be the property they were seeking. On contacting Alan Oldham in March, he kindly agreed to search through his documents again. Ultimately he was to find, in very small script, the crucial piece of evidence, the wording "the property formerly known as Magdala House". This was contained in an Assent of Will, a document relating to the sale of the property in 1917. At long last they had the answer: 'Magdala House' is today the property known as 'Terriers Green House'.

THE BIRTHPLACE OF GEOFFREY de HAVILLAND, MAGDALA HOUSE, NOW RENAMED TERRIERS GREEN HOUSE. The group at the unveiling of a plaque ceremony on 27th July 2000, L to R, Stuart McKay, Cllr. Pam Priestley, ?, Mrs. Oldham, ?, Cllr. Bill Jennings, Chantal de Havilland, Rosemary Cox, Alan Oldham, Anne Essex (née de Havilland), Ron Hedges, Gp. Capt. John Cunningham, John Essex, Cllr. David Cox, Air Cdre. J. Greswell, ?, Martin Cook, Jo. Tiddy, Dave Scott.

Photo - Dave Marriot / WDC.

Almost two years had passed since the start of this search. With its successful end a meeting was held in the Wycombe District Council offices in late March 2000. Those present included Jo Tiddy, Dave Scott and Stuart McKay of the de Havilland Moth Club. Their objective, to consider how best to commemorate the find which was, after all, an important piece of local history.

Jo was able to indicate that WDC would be willing to fund a commemorative plaque to denote the site of Sir Geoffrey de Havilland's birth. The plaque would be of green Welsh slate, designed and crafted by local letter carver Martin Cook. This was to be another of the commemorative plaques erected to honour the District's famous citizens, a scheme started in 1993 by WDC to ensure that future generations can inherit a tangible reminder of their historic past. Stuart McKay was sure that some form of aerial display could be arranged, but significantly indicated that British Aerospace (into which the original de Havilland organisation had been absorbed) would welcome the opportunity to show their recognition of the contribution Sir Geoffrey had made to aviation. Stuart's approach to Ron Hedges of British Aerospace produced a most positive response. It was decided to form a

committee to include: the three originators; plus Ron Hedges (BAE Systems); Eddie Russell, Mike Bomford and Fiona Chandler (all of W.D.C.); Alan Oldham (owner of the property) and James Rattue (Curator, Wycombe Museum).

The Museum was chosen as the site for a reception after an unveiling ceremony at the house. It was agreed the most appropriate date would be Sir Geoffrey's birth date, 27th July. However, it would clash with the Farnborough Air Show that had been moved from its traditional early September date to that week in July. By delaying the unveiling ceremony until 7.30pm. it was found possible for the guests, many of whom were to be present at Farnborough that day, to fulfil their obligations before travelling to the ceremony at High Wycombe.

Representing the family that evening were Anne Essex, Sir Geoffrey's granddaughter, and Chantal de Havilland, his great granddaughter. Anne Essex performed the unveiling of the plaque and gave a short speech outlining the family history. Despite recent variable weather the evening of the 27th was perfect for the fly past* that immediately followed. This was a magnificent display by no less than fifteen de

Havilland aeroplanes, all of pre-war design, a remarkable sight and a great tribute to their designer.

*See Appendix 1 for details of participating aircraft.

Also present that evening was the entire flight crew of the historic maiden test flight of the DH 106 Comet. The late John ("Cats Eyes") Cunningham, Chief Test Pilot for the de Havilland Aircraft Co., who was the pilot on that day, the co-pilot, John Wilson, and the Flight Test Engineer, Tony Fairbrother. During the evening John Cunningham looked at John Wilson and remarked that at this very time, 18.17 hours on the 27th July 1949 (which was Sir Geoffrey de Havilland's 67th birthday) they had taken off in the world's first jet airliner. By what can only be considered an amazing coincidence, John Cunningham also shares this same birth date. Later that evening, he was to be presented with a birthday cake by Ron Hedges.

Many former de Havilland employees were in attendance at the champagne reception held after the unveiling ceremony, in a marquee in the grounds of the High Wycombe Museum. On display in the marquee were the King's Cup, won by Sir Geoffrey in 1935 in a DH 85 Leopard Moth, together with a scale model of a DH 98 Mosquito and photographs of wartime production of this aircraft in Wycombe's furniture factories. British Aerospace had commissioned a painting of the Mosquito especially for the occasion. This was presented to Wycombe District Council and now hangs proudly in their offices, a fitting tribute to the town which had produced so many of the important components of this aircraft during the Second World War. Framed prints of this painting were also presented to Dave Scott and Alan Oldham.

Today, not only is there a plaque mounted on the wall of Terriers Green House but the entrance to the new estate further along the A404 Amersham Road has been named 'DE HAVILLAND DRIVE'. The road from Terriers to Hazlemere was once part of the old toll road that went from Reading to Hatfield, where Sir Geoffrey was eventually to have the head office and Aircraft Division of what became the great de Havilland enterprise. Some of the old milestones along the route can still be found today. One of these on the stretch of road between Marlow and Bisham always seemed puzzling. On it is marked "37 miles to Hatfield"! Why Hatfield? Why would anyone on that stretch of road need to know how many miles it was to Hatfield?

SIR GEOFFREY DE HAVILLAND

27th July 1882 – 21st May 1965

CAPT. GEOFFREY de HAVILLAND STANDING AT THE SIDE OF A DH9.
Photo - WDC.

Though Geoffrey was born in Hazlemere in 1882, he and the family were soon on the move to Nuneaton, when his father was appointed vicar there; then in 1896, they moved to Crux Easton, a hamlet on the North Hampshire Downs, about seven miles south of Newbury. Even at the early age of fourteen, Geoffrey was keenly interested in engineering and helped his elder brother Ivon to install an electrical generating plant in their new house.

In 1900 Geoffrey enrolled at the Crystal Palace Engineering School where he designed a motor cycle powered by a 1.5hp engine he had built himself. He joined the drawing office at the Wolseley Tool and Motor Co. in Birmingham in 1905, but eventually became disillusioned with the motor industry when his interest started to turn to the new challenges in aviation. His maternal grandfather gave him £1,000 to pursue his declared intent to build an aeroplane – the sum had apparently been willed to him anyway. Geoffrey then embarked on the project with his friend Frank Hearle in a workshop in Fulham.

By November 1909 his first machine was ready to test. A site at Seven Barrows, not far from Crux Easton, was chosen. Today a commemorative plaque identifies the location. Ground running and taxiing eventually convinced him that with a determined effort he could get it airborne. During this first attempt, he stalled the aircraft by lifting the nose too quickly, the aircraft reared up and then crashed to the ground. Luckily he escaped without serious injury. His machine was not so fortunate – the sudden stress had caused the wings to collapse, the fuselage had splintered into many pieces on impact and only the engine seemed to have remained intact. This setback did not deter him: he had learned from this initial experiment that the aircraft had the power to lift off the ground. With Frank Hearle, he returned to his workshop in Fulham more convinced than ever that they could build an aircraft that would fly.

On completion of the second machine, he travelled once again with Frank to Seven Barrows to resume testing; this time he was blessed with success. Slowly and carefully he flew further and higher, learning as he went how to control the new machine. This was the way with many of the early pilots: steadily and sensitively progressing, they learnt to fly the hard way, with only their growing experience as their teacher.

This perseverance eventually created a good pilot with a reliable machine, yet by now the money had all but run out: there was no means to promote the machine to the few people who might be persuaded to buy one at that time. It looked as if they had come to the end of the project. His good friend and assistant Frank and he had no permanent jobs, how could they carry on?

Then by chance, whilst attending the Olympia Aero Show of 1910, he met an old engineering friend, Fred Green. Fred was to be instrumental in finding an opening for them at Farnborough, at that time the Army Balloon Factory, where Fred was employed. An arranged meeting with Mervyn O'Gorman, the Superintendent there, resulted in Farnborough's purchase of his machine for £400 and employment for Frank as a mechanic and himself to supervise development of his own machine and other aircraft design work.

Though this appointment was a welcome break, with O'Gorman firmly backing them with his own belief that the aeroplane would eventually be superior to other methods of flying, other political forces were to prove overwhelming and aeroplane design at Farnborough was for a time stopped (for the second time). Today O'Gorman is recognised as an enthusiastic and far-sighted man, well capable of managing the task of researching and developing aircraft at that time. Others, including those who were more intent on ridicule and those in the emerging aircraft industry, who were envious of the growth of this establishment, were eventually responsible for the War Office implying he was no longer required. Yet it was during his term as superintendent there that aeroplane research and development had restarted and the Army Balloon Factory was renamed the Royal Aircraft Factory.

In January 1914, with the changing ideas at Farnborough, the Aeronautical Inspection Directorate (A.I.D.) had come into being as an independent organisation. De Havilland seemed the obvious choice as the Inspector of Aircraft, under Colonel Fulton. But he did not enjoy this period, feeling wasted in such a role, being cut off from designing, building and flying aircraft and the satisfaction he gained from this activity. His resignation came soon after a chance meeting with George Holt Thomas at Farnborough in early May of that year. This was probably the most important meeting he was to ever make. Since 1912, Holt Thomas had been manufacturing the French Farman Biplanes under licence at his firm "The Aircraft Manufacturing Company Ltd" at Hendon.

It was de Havilland's approach to this man, with the suggestion that he could design aircraft for him, that led to a further discussion, culminating in a contract being signed on 23rd May 1914, to become effective on 2nd July of that year. With a salary of £600 per year, de Havilland was again designing aircraft. With this company during the First World War we see the emergence of the first aircraft designs that carried what were to become the famous D.H. initials.

GEORGE HOLT THOMAS

How much do we know of George Holt Thomas today? Not enough really: from what we do know he seems a remarkable man, multi-talented and one of the early pioneers of aircraft manufacturing. He was born on 31st March 1870* in Brixton, London, the seventh son of William Luson Thomas, who was a newspaper proprietor and founder of the "Graphic Weekly Illustrated" and "Daily Graphic" newspapers in London. George Holt Thomas was privately educated at Queen's College, Oxford and in 1899 joined his father's business on the staff of the "Graphic Weekly Illustrated". Eventually he became a director of the business and extended it to include two more publications, which he himself founded, the "Bystander" and the "Empire Illustrated", publications centred on promoting the British Empire and British products.

*Ref. GRO, Births index – registered on 3rd May 1870.

GEORGE HOLT THOMAS.

His marriage at the parish church at Ightham in Kent to Gertrude Healey, a widow, is recorded on 19th April 1894. She was the youngest daughter of Thomas Oliver F.R.I.B.A., of Newcastle-upon-Tyne.

In 1906 he retired from the position of Director and General Manager of the printing company to follow his growing interest in aviation. Soon he was to become deeply involved in the new industry and was responsible for organising the first British flying display at Blackpool in 1909. Later that year he brought the French aviator Paulhan to the Brooklands and Sandown Park aviation displays and played a leading role in other aviation events of the time. In 1912 he started the "Aircraft Manufacturing Company Ltd." (A.M.C.). His initial object, using his own money, was to produce the French Farman biplanes under licence, convinced that Britain would be exposed to many dangers if those in Government continued to ignore the newly developing industry. He also obtained the rights to manufacture what were considered two of the finest aero engines of the time, the French "Gnome" and "Le Rhone" engines, production of these being carried out at the firm of Peter Hooker Ltd. Unfortunately he received little or no official backing or recognition for his endeavours.

An article submitted to "The Aeroplane" of the time (1917) by Mr. C. L. Freeston outlined his achievements, detailed by someone who understood them well. To quote: "No one has done more to develop aviation from every practical point of view than Mr. G. H. Thomas, the founder of the Aircraft Manufacturing Company. His interest in the movement was primarily journalistic, and began in 1906, when as director of the 'Graphic' and 'Daily Graphic' newspapers he offered a prize of £1,000 for a straight flight of one mile. Later in Paris he met with Henry Farman and through him became convinced that sustained flight was possible, given an engine able to perform in flight for a minimum of five minutes. He followed all the experimental stages until 1908, when Henry Farman won the Archdeacon prize for fluttering around a course of one millometre. *(This is the word used in the article, whether it means one mile or one kilometre, is unknown.)*

After the first Aviation meeting at Reims in 1909, Mr. Holt Thomas never left the public or War Office alone, not only by talking or writing, but by practical demonstrations through which he sought to impress all with the possibilities of flight. The service he thus rendered to the cause of flying, even before he became head of his great aircraft construction company, was immeasurable and priceless. He foresaw the necessity of military aviation and stated that it had been just as evident in 1910 as it is today [1917], and had at the time endeavoured unsuccessfully to get other firms interested in aircraft making to take up the matter. Eventually, in 1911, he started building the Farman machines (in which he had great faith) under licence. This was the start of the Aircraft Manufacturing Company."

In 1917 it is mentioned in the Bucks Free Press that he was residing locally in Wooburn Green, and was a neighbour of Mr. Walter Healey, the Chairman of the Wycombe Federation of Furniture Manufacturers. Was it Mr. Healey's influence that helped to get many of the urgently required wooden aircraft parts made by the furniture firms in this town? They certainly had the expertise required for such work.

By 1918, with the war over, we find that Holt Thomas had already moved to North Dean House at North Dean and was devoting his energies to dairy farming and raising a herd of prize-winning Friesian cattle. Locally respected and a generous employer, he did much to help the village. Yet in 1926 we find the first signs that all is not well. Holt Thomas decided to sell his herd "due to circumstances completely altered by the aftermath of war". In 1928 the estate was unsuccessfully offered at auction, as many lots remained unsold. He died on 1st January 1929 at Cimiez, France with some speculation as to the cause of his death.

His wife died less than three weeks later. There were no children and it would appear that the remainder of the estate was soon disposed of. His heir was a Mr. Noel Thomas, from whom the Memorial Hall and field were purchased by a board of trustees for North Dean, after his death.

These two men, Geoffrey de Havilland and George Holt Thomas had a great influence on High Wycombe's furniture industry in the First War years as will be shown in the following chapters.

ASTLEY'S BIRDLING MONOPLANE AT SAUNDERTON.

BFP 4th Aug. 1911.

MR HENRY DELAVEL ASTLEY LANDS HIS AEROPLANE AT SAUNDERTON SATURDAY 29th JULY 1911

It was the following Friday that a full report of this incident appeared in the Bucks Free Press giving information of the aeroplane that had landed in Mr. Saunder's meadow at Saunderton. The pilot was Mr. Henry Delavel Astley, flying his 50 h.p. Birdling Monoplane. This was essentially a copy of the Bleriot XI aeroplane, built by the Universal Aviation Company who had an office in Piccadilly, London, though it would seem they operated from Shed No. 17 at Brooklands. Two of these aeroplanes were built there. Astley, as their chief pilot, was flying one of these attempting to win a £10,000 prize offered by the Daily Mail. This stage of the competition was from Nottingham to Brooklands. The trip had not been without difficulties, and having arrived over Saunderton, he decided to land owing to the renewed strength of the wind. He then proceeded to London, as he explained, on some other

business, leaving the aircraft in the field. It certainly attracted a great deal of local attention during the weekend, as he did not resume the journey until early on Monday morning.

Mr. Astley was a Buckinghamshire man, the last of the line of ancestral owners of Chequers Court, or as we more familiarly know it today as just "Chequers". It had passed from the Russell family to the Astley family by marriage, towards the end of the 19th. century. The Astleys never took up residence, preferring to let the property, firstly to the Clutterbuck family, followed by the last people to take a lease on the property, Mr. and Mrs. Arthur Lee. Arthur Lee was a politician and his wife Ruth, an American heiress. Later they became Lord and Lady Lee of Fareham.

Astley was killed on the 27th September the following year whilst giving a flying display at the show grounds of the Royal Ulster Agricultural Society. After his death the property was purchased by Ruth Lee and her sister, who then gave it to Arthur Lee. In 1917, as theirs was a childless marriage, they decided to leave it to the nation. Eventually in 1921, by the Chequers Estate Act 1917, it was handed over, to become the country residence for the Prime Minister of the day. In the long gallery of the house, a stained glass window bears the inscription:

'THIS HOUSE OF PEACE AND ANCIENT MEMORIES WAS GIVEN TO ENGLAND AS A THANK OFFERING FOR HER DELIVERANCE IN THE GREAT WAR OF 1914-1918 AS A PLACE OF REST AND RECREATION FOR HER PRIME MINISTERS FOREVER.'

ASTLEY SEATED IN HIS BIRDLING MONOPLANE 1912.

COLONEL CODY COMES TO DOWNLEY

On Friday 20th September 1912 the Bucks Free Press carried a report of an event that had created great interest and excitement on the previous Saturday around the town of High Wycombe. On the 14th September 1912, Samuel Franklin Cody, one of this country's leading aviators, had landed his aeroplane in a field near Downley. To most people the sight of an aeroplane was still something very unusual.

With the passing of time, additions, exaggerations and errors have often crept into this story, so for reasons of accuracy this report is included here in full. The original needs no embellishment. Told as it was, it also gives us a remarkable insight into the man himself. Remember, at this time there were very few aeroplanes. On the 16th October 1908, only four years before, Cody himself had been the first to fly a powered aeroplane in Great Britain.

His flight is also mentioned in 'Flight' magazine of 21st September 1912 along with a very interesting in-depth article about Cody and his aeroplanes.

The Bucks Free Press article of Friday 20th September 1912

COLONEL CODY FLIES FROM FARNBOROUGH TO DOWNLEY

THOUSANDS VIEW A PRIZE BIPLANE

'A Splendid Flight.'

Shortly before eight o'clock on Saturday morning last, residents of the Wycombe district had an opportunity of obtaining a fine view of a biplane soaring through the air. The noise of the engine could be heard for some time before the biplane came into view. Hundreds of persons saw the biplane soar over the Wycombe Valley and go in the direction of Downley, where the aviator came down – in Mannings Field (then occupied by a Mr. Wm. Field), between Downley and Cookshall Farm. It was found that the pilot of the biplane was Colonel Cody – one of the most successful of our army airmen – he had his elder son, Mr Leon Cody, as passenger.

CODY'S AEROPLANE IN MANNINGS FIELD AT DOWNLEY, 14[IH] SEPTEMBER .1912.

BFP. 20th Sept. 1912.

IN MANNINGS FIELD ON SUNDAY, CODY'S AEROPLANE STANDS SHELTERED BY A CLUMP OF TREES. IN THE STRAW BOATER IS MR GREENWAY, THEN THE OWNER OF THE GROCER'S STORE ON THE CORNER OF HUGHENDEN AVENUE.

Photo - Mrs. Oliver (Daughter of Mr. Greenway).

Colonel Cody had flown from Farnborough (near Aldershot) to Downley in three-quarters of an hour. (A distance of 27 miles.) He was en - route for Cambridge, where during this week he has been taking part in manoeuvres. From a brief statement made by Mr. Leon Cody, it was gathered that at a height of 1,000ft, the wind was very cold and gusty, and that when Colonel Cody came lower down, the biplane ran into a thick bank of mist. As there had been discovered something wrong with the compass, he deemed it advisable to 'settle' (land). The biplane was a prize machine, with a 120 h.p. engine and weighed close to two tons. It was fitted up to carry four persons, but it can be made to carry eight.

When it became known that Colonel Cody was the aviator, and he was stopping at Downley for some hours, there was a big influx of visitors to the district. Mannings Field was a fine spot in which to settle, and it afforded thousands an opportunity of viewing the biplane. The Mayor of Wycombe (Mr. R. T. Graefe) was one of those early on the scene, and later on he entertained the distinguished aviator.

Colonel Cody left Wycombe shortly before 11 a.m. for Highbury Hill, where, during the day there was a rally of the Islington Local Association of Boy Scouts. Addressing the Scouts, Colonel Cody said he was very proud of the distinction conferred upon him by their invitation. He proceeded to relate the many-sided character of his life and how ultimately he had interested the army, through Sir John French, in his man flying kites. He also spoke of his exploits in the air, mentioning that he had flown round England with a big machine and a weak engine. It was with that discarded biplane, he said, that he had won the military competition this year. (Cheers). "I knew all along I would succeed," he continued, "but I could not get others to believe it."

"I am setting an example to you because I want you to see that the man or boy who tries hard will succeed. There should be no such word as failure in the heart of a Briton. (Cheers). I hope to see aeroplanes used by boy scouts in the protection of the British Nation in war. I don't want to see war, it is a wicked word, which conveys misery, poverty, crime, plunder and bloodshed, and we should avoid warfare all we can. If you get the best aeroplanes in the world no other country will attempt war against you, because in my opinion the aeroplane will rule the world within another ten years."

During Colonel Cody's absence until Sunday, Mr. Leon Cody remained in charge of the biplane. The weather being almost summer-like, induced many to make the journey to Downley. The machine was roped off in Mannings field and a charge for admission was made, - 2d for adults and 1d for children. The Mayor, who always has a thought for charitable objects, suggested that the proceeds should be devoted to the Wycombe Cottage Hospital, and no doubt this will be seriously considered by Mr. Field.

It was expected that Colonel Cody would resume his journey to Cambridge on the Saturday evening, and this fact caused the crowd to grow to considerable dimensions. Those who made the journey however, were doomed to disappointment. On Sunday the weather was even more genial than the previous day. Spectators were present almost as soon as it was daylight. Many tarried in the vicinity almost the whole of the day – evidently intending to see the start, which was delayed until about 5.30 in the evening.

Before leaving Colonel Cody briefly addressed the assembly. He thanked the Mayor for his great kindness, and then went on to say that he was delighted with the situation and delighted in the way the spectators had behaved. He could honestly say he had never received such kind treatment before. Colonel Cody then asked the spectators to stand clear, and promised to give them a fine view of the biplane, which he ultimately did. The biplane rose gracefully, and then went off at a terrific speed in a northerly direction, and was soon lost from sight. Colonel Cody landed safely at Cambridge. Those who had made the journey to Downley had their patience rewarded by seeing what was on all sides agreed to be a splendid exhibition of flying.

SAMUEL FRANKLIN CODY

Who was Cody? How had he become involved in the construction and flying of those early aeroplanes in which he achieved so much success? After his arrival in England he soon established himself as a fine showman. With his waxed moustache, Stetson, cowboy boots and riding his fine white horse he soon became a well-known stage figure.

"COLONEL" CODY".

Born in Texas, U.S.A., he was then named Samuel Franklin Cowdery. While still in the U.S.A., he had been, according to the records, buffalo hunter, cattle drover, gold prospector and a Wild West Showman. At that time, he would seem to have been more an adventurer than the innovator that he soon became within the aviation fraternity. He also developed a keen interest in the building and flying of kites, learning the basics from a Chinese cook during his time as a cattle drover. It was the development of this interest that would eventually lead him to greater things.

Arriving in Britain in 1889, he set up a base in Farnborough to sell horses. With a local girl, Lela Davis (with whom he set up home), he devised what became his highly successful 'Klondyke Nugget' Wild West sharp-shooting act, which they took around the British music hall scene. Sometimes he was billed as the son of the legendary Buffalo Bill Cody (ever a showman, it did him no harm not to correct this error). With the success of this show and the extra financial stability this provided, he was able to embark on experiments with his giant kites, including one designed to tow a small boat across the English Channel. He achieved this remarkable journey in 1903, in a time of 13 hours.

With this type of activity it is hardly surprising that he was to be noticed by the British Navy and Army. Eventually they sought his help to investigate the use of man carrying kites as observation platforms, giving him the post of Chief Kite Instructor with the Royal Engineers at the Balloon Factory, Farnborough. His man carrying kites were successful: even his wife was carried aloft, becoming the first woman to do this.

Unfortunately for Cody this project was soon to be discontinued. A kite observation platform was far too weather-dependent to be a practical proposition. His next commission was to help build a powered dirigible (airship) – the Nulli Secundus, which made its maiden voyage in 1907. After this, with £50 given him by the War Office for the purpose, he designed and built his first aeroplane, the British Army Aeroplane No.1. His first recorded flight in this machine was on 16th October 1908. It was a mixture of success and failure; he travelled 1,390ft. at a height of 50ft. before crashing to the ground trying to avoid a clump of bushes while landing. He had proved it would fly. Cody had become the first man officially recorded to fly a practical powered aeroplane in Britain.

At this point the War Office decided to withdraw its financial support and he was sacked. Unfortunately they were unconvinced there was any future in the project. It would be two years later before the War Office would reconsider their opinion on this issue. Another episode in our aviation history would start to unfold when in December 1910, Geoffrey de Havilland and his brother-in-law F. T. Hearle were taken onto the staff at Farnborough to continue the Army Aeroplane project. This story is best covered for those interested in Sir Geoffrey de Havilland's autobiography, 'Sky Fever'.

Cody must have been devastated by the decision: his first aeroplane had flown, he realised it had potential and knew that he could improve on what he had so far achieved. Time was to prove this very capable man was not the type to give up – he knew that he could do better. As an act of generosity he was allowed to keep the aeroplane, have the engine on loan and continue his flight trials at the far end of Laffan's Plain. Yet even this was criticised by the finance department of the War Office. Those chair-borne warriors objected at the likely cost of the coal. In their ignorance they thought he was using a steam engine to power his plane. How is it that people, who can be seen to be so far out of touch with reality, are allowed to make such decisions?

With a reconstructed version of the British Army Aeroplane No.1, re-named as the Cody Biplane No.1 (the original Flying Cathedral), he was to achieve a world record cross-country flight of 40 miles in September 1909. This was only two months after Bleriot had made his epic flight across the English Channel, a distance of just 24 miles. Cody took British citizenship at the first British aviation meeting at Doncaster in October of that year.

He continued with re-designing and improving through a series of aeroplanes, during which time he won the Michelin Trophy four times, setting many new records along the way. Money was always tight, misfortunes and problems many, however nothing could have been worse than when the two aeroplanes he had entered for the Military Trials in August 1912, (his Cody No.III biplane and his No.IV monoplane), were both damaged beyond repair early in July of that year. Against all odds, with his small team of helpers, he managed to build another biplane. Using many of the parts salvaged from the remains of the two crashed aeroplanes, he had his Cody No.V ready in time for the trials at Larkhill. He flew there on the 31st July, the last qualifying day. His team of helpers followed on their bicycles – even Wackett, a man of seventy years, made the sixty-mile journey on his tricycle – such was their enthusiasm and belief in this man. On arrival they found they had to sleep in the packing cases in which some of the other aeroplanes had arrived. Fitted with his ever-reliable 120h.p. Austro-Daimler engine, the Cody won both the British and International sections, and a well-earned £5,000 prize money. He had beaten them all.

It was in the following month that Cody was to make his landing at Downley, while flying to Hardwick Camp near Cambridge to take part in the army manoeuvres the following week. During this event King George V requested that Cody demonstrate his aeroplane for him. While in conversation, the King several times addressed him as Colonel Cody. From then on Colonel Cody it was, even though Cody had no such military title. There can be little doubt that in previous years, as a civilian advisor with his position as Chief Kite Instructor to the Army, he had earned the respect of those who worked with him. Many considered he had earned and deserved some such recognition.

One month later, with an all British 100h.p. Green engine installed in place of his 120h.p. Austro-Daimler, he entered the All-British section of the Michelin Trophy. He won the trophy, for the fourth time. Immediately afterwards the aeroplane was refitted with the Austro-Daimler engine and passed to the Royal Flying Corps (R.F.C.). This was to fulfil part of an order that he had received for two aeroplanes after winning the Military Trials at Larkhill in August. This aeroplane was displayed at the April 1913 Aero Show at Olympia. A notice alongside indicated that by then it had flown some 7,000 miles. During 1912/13 an identical aeroplane was built for service with the RFC and was used by Nos. 2 and 4 Squadrons.

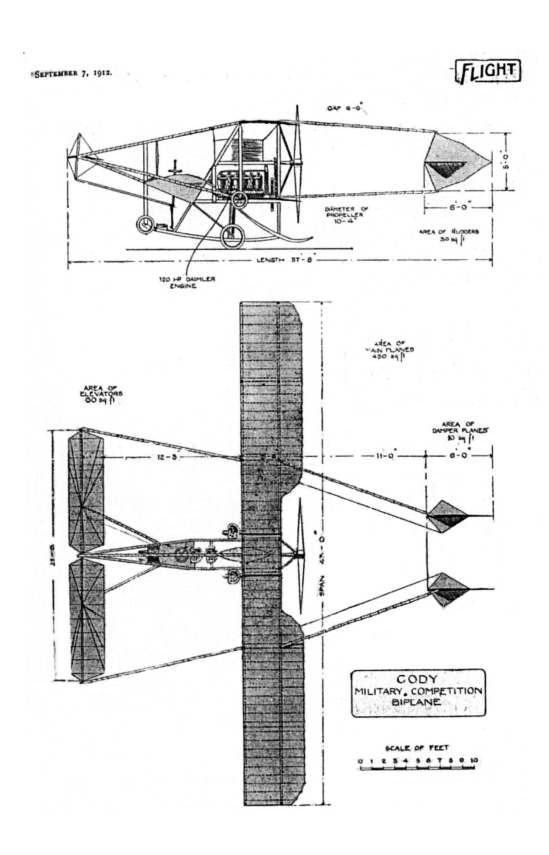

PLAN AND ELEVATION OF THE CODY BIPLANE THAT WON FIRST PRIZE AT THE MILITARY TRIALS IN 1912.

FLIGHT MAGAZINE Sept. 12th 1912.

TODAY CODY'S AEROPLANE CAN BE SEEN ON DISPLAY AT THE SCIENCE MUSEUM AT SOUTH KENSINGTON.

Tragically, on 7th August 1913 at the age of 53, Cody was killed while testing his latest No.VI water plane at Farnborough. He and his passenger were seen to fall from the aeroplane as it broke up in mid-air. Later investigation would seem to indicate that the propeller had shattered and caused other serious structural damage. So died a man who was considered to be one of the best pilots of the time, not through a lack of flying skill, but by an unfortunate structural failure.

Colonel Cody's funeral on 11th August 1913 was held with full military honours. Several regiments and the Navy were represented. A crowd of many thousands lined the route from his home at Ash Vale, near Farnborough, to the Military Cemetery at Aldershot. This man was their hero of the air, a man considered to be the father of British flying. He was the first civilian to be buried there. His wife was also later to be buried alongside.

There are several books written about Cody, his life and achievements. Recommended reading for those interested: *Pioneer of the Air*, by G. A. Bloomfield, and *The Flying Cathedral, by* Arthur S. Gould Lee. Both give an insight into this remarkable and determined man and those early years of flying.

OUR FIRST AIRFIELD

SAUNDERTON 1913

A small part in a large event during September 1913

THE BATTLE OF BOOKER

In a Bucks Free Press article of the 19th September 1913 we find mentioned what was probably the first airfield or landing strip established in this area, the Army Aviation Station at Saunderton. In it we are told the aviation quarters were on Mr. Anderson's grounds at The Rectory Farm, Saunderton.

Here, many residents from Saunderton and Princes Risborough, keen to see the aerial activities, were able to witness some fine exhibitions of flying skill performed by pilots of the Royal Flying Corps. The aeroplanes were also regularly seen flying over the towns of High

Wycombe, Marlow and Princes Risborough, as they took part in the Army Manoeuvres in the area. At one stage an army airship was seen passing over High Wycombe; having circled the town it then headed away towards the south-west.

A HENRY FARMAN ARMY BIPLANE APPROACHING THE LANDING FIELD AT SAUNDERTON

BFP Sept. 1913

The article was mainly describing to its readers in some detail the activities of many army units that had arrived in the surrounding areas of High Wycombe. Our section was in fact just a small local part of a much larger military exercise that was to cover an area stretching from beyond Rugby in the north to what would appear to be a line just south of the River Thames. The main battle is outlined in another article published in the Bucks Free Press in the previous month, on the 15th August 1913 (complete with a map of the area covered). It was to take place from 22nd to the 26th September. This epic battle was preceded by many skirmishes in the outlying districts as the regiments involved took up their positions.

In this area part of the Brown (southern) Army, the First and Second Aldershot Divisions under their Commander, Sir Douglas Haig, was to move up from Aldershot, initially to take up positions at Waltham St. Lawrence and Haynes Hill. This force, 20,000 strong plus all their transport and equipment, stretched 8 miles along the road as they moved off towards their objective. From here they were able to place 15,000 men strategically along the south bank of the Thames from Henley to Marlow, intending to cross the river to engage the White (northern) Army who had fallen back to take up defensive positions to the north of the Thames. Both Marlow and Henley bridges were to be considered destroyed, so crossings were to be made over pontoon bridges constructed by the Royal Engineers.

The opposing White Army's Guards Brigade at Bovingdon Green, under General Briggs, were joined by the Cavalry Brigade consisting of Dragoons, Hussars, Field Artillery and Engineers. From here they moved out to take up defensive positions, dug in on a line from Seymour Court, just above the Thames valley at Marlow, to Frieth with the cavalry units at its flanks. As the battle commenced, some aircraft were seen observing the scene below. One report states that one of the Brown Army aircraft performed a useful service by dropping an urgent message almost at the feet of General Lomax, one of the commanders.

More interest was also raised at Hurley during the week with the arrival of three aeroplanes landing at a camp site between Rose Hill and the river. One had flown all the way from Montrose in Scotland, known to be the base at that time of No. 2 Squadron R.F.C. (the squadron that the young Capt. de Havilland was to join for a short time at the beginning of the First World War). The other two had arrived from Farnborough. Colonel Seely, the War Minister, on arrival at this site, went up for a short flight in a Henry Farman biplane piloted by Lieut. Stockford of the Royal Flying Corps. It was Colonel Seely who had imposed the controversial ban on monoplane flying in the army after a series of fatal accidents that seemed to indicate the monoplane structure was unsafe.

Throughout the week as many as five or six Army aeroplanes could be seen daily in the area intently observing the manoeuvres below. This activity was one of the earliest instances of using aeroplanes to observe the movements of troops on the ground below and then passing this information back to their own troops – probably the first time that the British Army had seriously considered the use of aeroplanes in this way and on such a large scale. They were the first Air Observation Post (A.O.P.) aircraft as they later became known.

One of the army commanders wryly commented that, with this new ability, the chance of surprising the enemy in future would be greatly reduced. An attempt to eliminate this threat would soon follow, though, during the First World War. Every chance would be taken to shoot them down as they flew low over the ground to observe enemy positions. They flew higher to avoid the ground fire, which led to the start of those deadly air battles, armed aircraft against armed aircraft. How sadly we can now look back at Cody's vision, that the aeroplane would bring hope for peace.

The Old Rectory House, which today stands between the two rail lines that cross the Upper Icknield Way, gives an approximate location of the site of the aviation ground, which was in the adjacent fields stretching towards the A4010.

Even today they look well suited for a landing field. (O/S 1:50,000 sheet 165, reference SP 799 013.)

It was during this battle that land on the Halton estate, owned by Mr. Alfred de Rothschild, was offered for the army's use. An extra field was then cleared of sheep to be used as an airstrip by the Army Flying Corps. On Thursday 18th September four aircraft from 3 Squadron landed here, to be followed next day by the rest of the squadron. This airstrip eventually became RAF Halton. With great foresight, Lord Trenchard created the air force's apprentice school here, which over the following years started the training of many young men for their future in the service. The RAF Hospital, also built here, provided a medical centre not only to current members of the air force, but to all who had served in the RAF. Continuing Government cutbacks eventually forced the closure of this once very valuable asset.

LOUIS BLERIOT 1872-1936

Louis Bleriot made history on the 25th July 1909 when he succeeded in crossing the English Channel with a flight in a heavier than air machine of his own design, the Bleriot No. XI monoplane. This epic flight was probably the turning point for many who had poured scorn on those who tried to fly such weird contraptions. In 1910, Bleriot established an aircraft company in England. With the outbreak of war in 1914 it was rapidly expanded, with further manufacturing facilities at Addlestone, Surrey.

BLERIOT'S BOURNE END RESIDENCE

Two years later, in 1916, he purchased a residence, called New York Lodge, on the bank of the River Thames at Bourne End, just downstream of Andrews boatyard. It is described as having 21 bedrooms, 5 reception rooms, a winter garden and lovely grounds running down to a boathouse at the river's edge. It was previously owned by Mr. George A. Kessler, who was reputed to have spent the sum of £30,000 remodelling the original late Victorian house. He was an American millionaire, involved with importing champagne. In 1915 Kessler was returning from America on the Lusitania when the vessel was struck and sunk by a German torpedo. He survived the experience but he never returned to England and the house was put up for sale.

THE SITE OF BLERIOT'S RESIDENCE JUST BELOW ANDREWS BOATHOUSE. The arrow at the bottom of the picture indicates the propeller flower bed.

Photo - Brian Wheals.

A great deal of work was still required on the property and it was not until April 1919 that Cherau, the Manager of the Bleriot factory at Brooklands, reported, "Bourne End will be ready soon." At some stage it was renamed Riversdale House.

In the summer of 1919, Bleriot left all the financial problems inherent in aircraft manufacturing at the time to spend a holiday in Britain at his lovely house in Bourne End. His wife recollected: -

"It was lively and amusing, with servicemen back from the war organising boating parties to go up the Thames. Our house was well known, and people knew that Bleriot was there, so they came and serenaded him under our windows. A party of English airmen, all aces from the War, had rented a cottage on one of the nearby backwaters, and they came to dine or play tennis or bowls several times a week. We had an electrically driven boat that could take twenty or thirty people. We would set out in the afternoon and have tea on board. The men wore bathing costumes under their clothes, and late in the evening they would go to the stern and jump in, then follow us home swimming."

Bleriot had also made arrangements for his children to go to college in England.

NEW YORK LODGE

Photo - Brian Wheals.

After the War the finances of Bleriot's company went from bad to worse. Creditors seized the factory in 1926. Around that time a major fire destroyed New York Lodge; all that remained was sold for only £2,000, to help pay off his creditors.

During Bleriot's occupation of New York Lodge, local accounts tell of a special flowerbed that was set out in the grounds depicting a propeller. The aerial photograph above, taken in 1935, still shows this feature.

CHAPTER 2

1914 – 1918. THE GREAT WAR YEARS

These were the years that established the aeroplane – it was no longer something that could be ignored or ridiculed. The emerging manufacturing industry was given great impetus by the need that had now become obvious: it was an effective new tool of war. Many had foretold that a war was inevitable; some also foresaw ways the aeroplane could be developed and would be used to advantage in such conflicts. It is well to remember that those who would be our enemies were also well capable of producing aircraft, some already in advance of our own. They would soon prove their effectiveness. This urgent need was the driving force behind the development of many new military aircraft over the next months and years of war, throughout which the balance of air power passed several times from one side to the other as new and more lethal aircraft were developed. Initially used for observation, it was not long before they were armed with guns and bombs enabling them to attack the enemy on the ground as well as each other in the air.

When war commenced, Geoffrey de Havilland, who had joined the Royal Flying Corps Reserve whilst at Farnborough, was immediately taken from his employment at Aircraft Manufacturing Company to report to Farnborough. He was then sent directly to Montrose as an officer on war duty. His main duty was patrolling the North Sea in an outdated, unarmed Bleriot monoplane looking for German submarines. By the end of August he was returned to his design office at Hendon, where he would obviously be better employed, designing new and more lethal aircraft for the RFC. His first design, the DH 1, was a two-seat reconnaissance biplane; however the War Office urgently needed an aircraft of higher performance to counter the threat of the new German Fokker E1 Eindekker. The Eindekker was the first aircraft to be fitted with a machine gun with interrupter mechanism, allowing the pilot to fire through the propeller arc. It had been creating havoc among the British aircraft. The DH 2 was essentially a scaled down, single seat fighter version of the DH 1. It was soon under construction; working on this continuously, the first flight was achieved on the 1st June 1915. This proved successful. Mass production was soon to provide the RFC with over 400 of these aircraft.

The DH 3, a twin engine bomber capable of reaching Berlin, their next project, had to be put aside to develop a new idea of a day bomber, the DH 4.

This was a great success. Faster than most of its contemporary fighters, it made its first flight in August 1916. The DH 4 and a later development, the DH 9, were built in large numbers, over 4,000. These played a major role with the RFC, the Royal Naval Air Service and, from the 1st April 1918, the newly formed Royal Air Force. In 1920, after the war, the DH 4 was to become the mainstay of the U.S. Army Air Corps. The U.S. Air Mail service was also equipped with these aircraft.

It certainly proved to be a very successful aircraft. Much of the work was done by sub-contractors, including many of Wycombe's furniture factories during those arduous war years.

A DH 9 AIRCRAFT

During this period there are other indications of High Wycombe's involvement with aircraft manufacture. With its furniture industry and expertise, it was a prime site from which to pick the men with the right skills. At first many of the local craftsmen had to move to the sites where aircraft were being manufactured. Airco at Hendon expanded greatly, but this was still insufficient to cope with the volume of work. Perhaps Holt Thomas had already realised it would be more expedient to take the work to the factories that were equipped to do such work, rather than continue with a policy of moving the workforce to his own factories. Whatever the reason, many local firms were soon to be producing aircraft components. Earliest references allude to wings being produced for the Maurice Farman biplane and the most likely recipient for these of course would have been Airco where they were being built under licence.

WYCOMBE'S NEW INDUSTRY

A group of local notables gathered together on 22nd November 1917 outside the works of W Skull, to celebrate a definite stage of progress in Wycombe's involvement in producing aircraft parts.
Back row, Mr H. Harvey; Mr. F. W. Burr; Mr. H. G. Parker (Vice Chairman of the Furniture Manufacturers Federation); Mr. H. T. Dickens (President of the High Wycombe and District Camber of Commerce); Mr. T. Kemp-Walton, ACIS; Mr. W. T. Barnes; Mr. A. C. Boorman, FCIS; Mr. F. Skull.
Middle row, Lieut. Bentley (Department of Aeronautical Supplies); Mr. W. Hollins; Mr. T. J. Northy; Mr. Percy Raffety, FSI; Mr. J. May; Mr. A. J. Clarke (Town Clerk); Mr. C. A. Skull; Mr. R. Ellis.
Front row, Mr. T. E. Ritchie, AMIEE, AMI Mech. E.; Mr. J. T. Ford (Sec. Local Branch Men's Union); Mr. W. H. Healey (Chairman of the Furniture Manufacturers' Federation); Mr F. H. Payne, (Managing Director of Wycombe Aircraft Constructors Ltd.); Councillor O. Haines (Mayor of Chepping Wycombe); Mr. C. F. Skull JP; Alderman Wharton (Deputy Mayor); Mr. C. W. Raffety JP.

Photo - BFP.

Mr. J. C. Lane, the owner of a furniture firm then in Abercrombie Avenue, had made a shrewd observation on the very first day of the war. He realised that people would have to do without furniture during the coming conflict, and war products would take priority. The thought occurred to him: if there was a war there would be wounded soldiers and therefore a need for hospital furniture. He immediately started to design for the production of these items and just a month later he was turning a large barracks into a hospital for wounded soldiers under a government contract. Throughout the war this was to be his speciality.

Like other local firms at the time, Lane's also became involved with producing aircraft parts. Interviewed about this he stated, "We were all involved in studying millimetres instead of inches, this was to comply with the exacting standards required by the inspectors, who were checking the components with various scientific and mathematical devices." Was this one of the first instances of our going metric? Airco would certainly be using metric units, as their main production had been building the French Farman biplanes, the RFC's main aircraft at the start of the war.

Other components mentioned were the wings for the Airco DH 4 and DH 9 at E. Gomme Ltd. in Leigh Street. Clapton Mill in Wooburn is mentioned as producing aircraft wings and propellers. Gomme's also had a separate factory producing propellers. An interesting comment found in a book about Wooburn during 1915 states, "An aeroplane, which alighted behind Hedge Mill, was left in the care of the local constable while the pilot visited Mr. Thornton

Smith at Clapton's Mill." No doubt the pilot had some urgent aircraft business to conduct.

Early in the war, demands on the whole of High Wycombe's furniture industry and its workforce were found to be having an adverse effect. They were still expected to provide many other requirements while their skilled workforce was being poached to work on aeroplane production elsewhere. As a typical example of these other demands – F. Parker & Sons (later to become Parker Knoll), who were already making parts for the Sopwith Pup and Camel aircraft in 1915 at their Uxbridge factory, were also asked to fulfil an order for 20,000 field kettle stands and 2,000,000 tent pegs.

AIRCRAFT WINGS FOR A DH 9 BEING
PRODUCED AT E. GOMME LTD.
Photo – BFP

Their manufacturing capacity was being stretched to the limit in also making chairs and tables to meet army demands and urgently needed hospital furniture. These demands, common throughout the town, were responsible for greatly unbalancing the workforce. As these items were only a robust but crude type of furniture, made by the less skilled workers, the 'Best Chairmakers', as they were known, were left with little work to do. The bosses were certainly not prepared to pay the higher rate they were entitled to for such menial tasks, but at the same time were unhappy with having to give up any of their more highly skilled work force. Yes, even in wartime there were industrial disputes. Remember that those 'Best

Chairmakers' who were still working would be those unfit for military service, either too old or some already returned to the industry, incapacitated in some way by the war.

Another local firm producing parts for Sopwith was William Birch. They also made parts for the Airco DH 4 and DH 9.

For the first time women found a new acceptance within the industry and were employed to do much of what was considered to be a man's work.

During the last two years of the war the Situations Vacant columns in the Bucks Free Press were continually full of adverts requiring cabinetmakers, joiners, woodworkers and their like for aeroplane work within many of the town's furniture factories. E. Gomme, Walter Skull, G. H. & S. Keen, H. Connelly, F. Parker, C. P. Vine, R. Tyzak and Thomas Glenister were all known to be helping with aircraft production at that time. Most of these were involved with work for the Airco DH 4. The firm of William Bartlett and Son were involved with making parts for Handley Page Ltd., these probably for the Handley Page 0/100 or 0/400 bomber aircraft. These enormous heavy bombers, with their 100 ft. wingspan, and endurance of eight hours, were capable of flying to the heart of Germany with a 2,000lb. (907kg.) bomb load. A factory that stood on the site of the present village hall in West Wycombe was another employed in making wings. These were assembled on the first floor of the building, and a new exit had to be cut through the wall to enable them to be lowered onto the transport below. Today, most of these firms are no longer with us, though for many years they had represented the backbone of our town's industry. All these firms were desperate to attract what remained of the town's skilled woodworkers.

Yet in 1917 another government appeal was made for a further 25% of craftsmen from the furniture industry to be selected to work on the manufacturing of aircraft elsewhere. How could they cope? One can only imagine what consternation this stirred up at the time.

In the B.F.P. of the 27th July 1917 is shown, (in the inimitable way that only a good local paper reporting the true local conditions can), the awkward situation that was developing and we can also observe the seeds of a new idea start to evolve – a new solution that could cope with what had become an intolerable situation for all involved. Once again one can feel a steadying hand as the situation is carefully outlined by a group formed to address this problem, so well led by Mr. W. H. Healey. Not for the first time nor the last was it to be his careful assessment of a situation that would show the way forward. The problem and its solution are stated so well.

There would be other times when this man's influence would guide the industry through difficult times, one being to establish a balanced wage agreement within the trade during another difficult time. His approach to this particular problem is evident in The Bucks Free Press article of 17th July 1917, as here related.

WYCOMBE'S SHORTAGE OF SKILLED WORKERS

POSSIBILITIES OF AEROPLANE WORK

A few weeks ago 'The Cabinet Maker' published some important information with regard to a scheme of National Service in the furniture trade. Reference was made to the constitution of a Central Joint Committee, the object of its appointment being to facilitate the release of workmen in the furniture industry from their ordinary class of labour, to enable them to be engaged on work of national importance, more especially upon aeroplane manufacture. The scheme was outlined by 'The Cabinet Maker' magazine in the following note: - "It is the aim of the committee that a proportionate number of workmen should be released from all factories and workshops upon a fair and reasonable basis, so that every district and firm will contribute a due quota of the number required. They suggest that 25% of the workmen in each district or town should be released for this urgent and pressing work of National Service, and earnestly appealed for the co-operation and assistance of both employers and employees. They urge that local joint committees should at once be formed in each district and town for this purpose, and arrangements made without delay for a joint meeting of employers and workmen's associations"

A Local Joint Committee for Wycombe and the district has now been formed, consisting of seven employers and an equal number of operatives in the furniture trade, with Mr. W. H. Healey as Chairman and Mr. W. Day as Vice-Chairman. Considering that 25% of the skilled workers now remaining in Wycombe are required for the manufacture of the wooden parts of aeroplanes, it is felt a very serious matter from the point of view of the town and its future, especially having regard for the already depleted state of the staffs in all the factories. A large proportion of the labour left in Wycombe is necessarily unskilled or semi-skilled. The skilled worker is, in fact, carrying the unskilled worker, and neither can get on without the other.

MR WALTER HENRY HEALEY, CHAIRMAN OF THE FURNITURE MANUFACTURERS' FEDERATION

Photo – BFP

The question arises: Does it not seem now that instead of the town parting with the remainder of its skilled workers, a determined effort should be made to ensure that this aeroplane work (as suggested above), shall be executed in Wycombe? It is a well known fact that Wycombe is regarded in the wood working industry as being in the front rank in respect of railway facilities, up to date machinery, and spacious and well equipped factories. Yet skilled men have gone in large numbers from the town and are at the present time doing precisely the class of work that could be executed in Wycombe.

The skilled workers of this town at the present moment undoubtedly feel that if the country's need is aeroplanes, they are only too ready and willing to devote their energies to that particular class of work. An important point urged is that, being men of expert knowledge and practical training, there is no need to separate them from their homes and take them away from their own benches and shops. It is not perhaps sufficiently realised that if the qualified skilled workers are taken, those who remain to keep the industry going have no reasonable opportunity of becoming skilled themselves.

The manufacture of aeroplane wings and parts is largely the cabinet maker's work and as there are a number of these skilled operatives still left in the town - men who are ineligible for military service, they could well superintend the new form of labour if it were introduced in our midst. It may be said that Wycombe has not the wood in stock suitable for aeroplane parts, but as the timber is specially imported for the purpose, there should be no insuperable difficulty in obtaining a supply to cope with the exigencies of the situation. If other towns obtain the necessary wood, surely Wycombe could at least be similarly treated. It is felt that the matter is so vitally important, from the point of view of the industry of the town that a special effort should be made by way of representation to the proper Authority in order to secure the retention of Wycombe's skilled workmen and the unskilled operatives also, to do work of the very first importance to the Nation and Empire. What is wanted is not individual effort and if employers and workers will only combine their forces, there is no reason why their joint action should not result in the attainment of that success which we all desire.

In this article we have seen the nettle grasped – somehow an answer had to be found. Behind all this political endeavour, Wycombe was fighting, with good reason, to stop the poaching of its skilled workforce. This would affect the town's ability for many years to come. There was, quite rightly, a fear that having been forced to let these men go, they might never return. The work must come to Wycombe. It is quite amazing how quickly the idea was developed, other ideas and offers soon materialised. The answer was to have within the town our own aircraft assembly factory, taking all parts produced here and completing the job of building aeroplanes.

Once again we are indebted to the Bucks Free Press of the time for their careful reporting of a scheme that offered a fine solution to the problem, one that would also bring great benefits to the town. To do it justice, this report is presented in full from the Bucks Free Press of 28th September 1917. At this time we were in the midst of the war. Decisions were made under great pressure, they had to succeed, no time for questioning what the future might eventually hold, only the will to make the best effort and do what was necessary for the great national purpose, to win the war at all cost.

A NEW INDUSTRY.
WYCOMBE, AN AEROPLANE CENTRE
GREAT SCHEME BROUGHT TO COMPLETION.

THE TOWN'S FUTURE, UNLIMITED POSSIBILITIES FOR EXPANSION

Coming events cast their shadow before them, says an old proverb. For some little time past there has been on the local horizon the signs of big events impending in the local industry, changes fraught with momentous issues with regard to the future of the town and district. In our issue of July

27th we referred to a call made upon the furniture trade to supplement its already large contribution to the fighting ranks of Britain by a further supply of labour to be used in the manufacture of aeroplanes, and the question was asked why a determined effort should not be made to bring the work to Wycombe, instead of transporting local workers away from their homes to other manufacturing areas.

It was pointed out that Wycombe would be an admirable centre in every way for the manufacture of aeroplane parts, possessing as it does skilled labour, up to date machinery and every other facility for the purpose. There is also a fully adequate railway system for the import of raw materials and the dispatch of the finished product. "The Cabinet Maker", the leading trade journal, afterwards devoted a couple of articles to the same subject, and gave indisputable reasons in favour of the project. Meanwhile local efforts were not idle. Mr. W. H. Healey, Chairman of the local Federation of Manufacturers took a very serious view of the constant drain upon the manpower of the town, worked hard in investigations and inquiries, and it was largely through his energy and foresight that contact was gained with influential channels through which the heads of the aviation world and the government authorities could be approached.

There was, of course much to be done before a scheme of such magnitude could be put into practice. Local circumstances had to be studied, and possible difficulties provided for, such as any unnecessary disturbance of existing industrial conditions. But any difficulties that arose vanished when a scheme of such inherent value to the community began to shape itself. Mr. Healey had much correspondence and many interviews before the proposition was ready for submission to the local federation.

One of the most important steps was the enlistment of the help of Mr. Holt Thomas, whose knowledge of aviation matters from a practical standpoint is unsurpassed by anyone in the country. Mr. Healey found Mr. Holt Thomas quite ready to fall in with any plans that would help forward the development of the town near which he resides, and his powerful aid was largely instrumental in bringing a practical scheme into existence.

THE PROJECT IN BEING

The stage of preliminary spadework had now passed, and that of definite result has been reached. A scheme has been launched that will have an enormous influence upon the future of Wycombe. It will be put into working order immediately, and it is not too much to say that its *ultimate effort will be a revolution in local conditions.*

Briefly summarised, the project now put upon a working basis is the formation of a powerful company, with adequate financial backing and large resources of practical skill and experience.

With the undertaking are associated some of the foremost figures in the great national work of aeroplane construction, and government sanction has been obtained for the important development in view. Local factories will be employed in the manufacture of aeroplane parts, and extensive premises will shortly be in readiness for the assembling of those parts and the final touches in construction.

THE SCHEME EXPLAINED TO THE LOCAL FEDERATION

The details of this far-reaching undertaking were explained to the members of the Wycombe Federation of Furniture Manufacturers, at a special meeting on the 20th September. Mr. W. H. Healey presided, and the keen interest that was felt in the subject was shown by the fact that every member of the federation was present – a circumstance unique in its history.

The Chairman introduced to the meeting Mr. F. H. Payne, a gentleman whose name and personality will mean much to the Wycombe of the future, for he is the Managing Director of the new undertaking.

Mr. Payne in a lucid and interesting address, referred to, in the first place the shortage of labour already apparent in Wycombe factories, secondly the prospect of a further depletion of 25% of workmen who were to be drawn away for aeroplane work. But he was able, he said, to lay before them a proposition that would not only enable Wycombe to keep its skilled labour under the protection of the Munitions Department, but would in all probability bring back to the town many who had already gone to other centres and introduce a new supply of labour, to the mutual advantage of employers and operatives. Mr. Healey their chairman had been in communication with Mr. Holt Thomas who was not only a neighbour of theirs, but was well known as the foremost figure in this country, if not in the world in regard to aeroplane construction. The result of negotiation and consultation had been the formation of a new company, with the title- WYCOMBE AIRCRAFT CONSTRUCTORS LIMITED.

MR. F. W. PAYNE. APPOINTED MANAGING DIRECTOR OF THE WYCOMBE AIRCRAFT CONSTRUCTORS.

Photo – BFP

Mr. Holt Thomas had for some time appreciated the opportunity offered by the factories and skilled labour at Wycombe, and he heartily welcomed the opportunity that now presented itself.

The difficulty had been to find someone with the necessary practical knowledge and experience to undertake the work of organisation. The moment Mr. Holt Thomas learned that he (the speaker) had relinquished his active association with the Grahame White Aviation Company (of which he had been for over two years the joint Managing Director), he approached him on the subject, with the result that he accepted the appointment of Managing Director of the company whose title he had given them. He assured them that he entered into the project with the greatest enthusiasm and the brightest hopes of success, and he might say that their plan had the full approval of Sir William Weir, the Controller of Aeronautical Suppliers.

The members of the federation would fully appreciate the urgent national need for aeroplanes and still more aeroplanes, and he was certain that from a patriotic point of view they would concur in anything that tended towards the increase of supply. He was sure, also, that they would be gratified to find how their own interest and those of their town coincided with that great national purpose.

Mr. Payne eloquently pictured the great possibilities for Wycombe arising out of the new industry. He was prepared immediately, under a contract already placed with the new company, to place among the various factories of the town orders to the value of – OVER FIFTY THOUSAND POUNDS.

This was only a small beginning. If the members of the federation and the trade generally were prepared to throw themselves heart and soul into the new enterprise, there was no reason why in the future, vast sums of money should not find their way into Wycombe though the medium of aeroplane construction.

There was no wish on the part of Mr. Holt Thomas or the new company to interfere with the controls of local factories or with existing conditions. All they desired was the cordial co-operation of the federation and the workmen's union in this great national work. They were desirous of affording to the manufactures the fullest possible assistance in the methods that would be necessary, and he took the opportunity of introducing to them Mr. Thomas E. Ritchie, A.M.I.Mech.E., A.M.I.E.E., an engineer of wide experience, who would be Resident General Manager of the company, Mr. T. Kemp Walton, A.C.I.S., A.L.A.A., who would be the Resident Secretary. A staff of qualified constructors would be available for the instruction and assistance of local labour in the technical details of the work entrusted to them. Three constructors would visit the factories and give any help that was needed. What he now had to suggest was that all the firms represented should supply full particulars of the accommodation, plant and labour available in their factories, and he would particularly call attention to the fact that a large proportion of the semi-skilled labour – male and female – would be employed. In conclusion, Mr. Payne expressed the keen desire felt by Mr. Holt Thomas and himself that the enterprise should receive the assistance and support it deserved, in the interest of the wood working industry of the town and of the nation at large. He ventured to claim that interest and support from all classes engaged in local industry, and he felt confident that the project would be welcomed in a spirit of appreciation and mutual co-operation.

Mr. Payne's address was followed by an informal discussion, during which many questions on points of detail were asked and satisfactorily answered.

Mr. Fred Skull then moved the following resolution:- that the best thanks of this meeting be given to the deputation, and that this federation welcomes the event of their company into Wycombe.

In doing so, Mr. Skull remarked that they meet on a most historic occasion, and as the representative of one of the oldest furniture factories in Wycombe, he was proud to have the opportunity of proposing a resolution that he believed would mark the beginning of a new era in the history of the town. He was in entire sympathy with the scheme that had been outlined that evening, and he felt certain that it embodied possibilities for the industrial progress of Wycombe the extent of which at the moment they could hardly estimate. The resolution was seconded by Mr. H. G. Parker, and was carried unanimously with acclamation.

A cordial vote of thanks to Mr. Payne and to Mr. Healey closed these formal proceedings.

Afterwards the majority of the members of the federation intimated their intentions of offering the facilities of their factories in furtherance of the company's enterprise.

WYCOMBE'S FUTURE: A GREAT AEROPLANE CONSTRUCTION CENTRE

Since the memorable meeting above recorded, promises of support have multiplied and the success of the project is fully assured. A moment's reflection is sufficient for comprehension of the vast possibilities opened to Wycombe and the district, The Managing Director of the new enterprise was good enough to accord an interview to the representative of this journal, in which some further details of interest were supplied.

Mr. Payne first paid a warm tribute to the practical help given by the Marquis of Lincolnshire, the principal land owner in the district, who with his usual desire to help forward any movement for the benefit of Wycombe, had offered every facility for the acquirement of a suitable site for the assembling shops that are to be erected. Negotiations have been concluded by which the Company will gain possession of 22 acres of land in Bell Field, on the western side of the town. On this convenient site extensive buildings will be erected. The plans are in the course of preparation, operations will begin immediately, and it is expected that in three or four months' time the sheds will be ready for occupation. Here the parts manufactured in local factories will be bought together for "assembly", and facilities will be furnished for what is *technically known as the "trimming" and "doping" of the wings and other component portions.*

The point that Mr. Payne is anxious to be clearly understood is that the Company has no intention of competing in any shape or form with the accustomed work of the local factories. "We are out to make aeroplanes not furniture," he emphatically stated.

To a query as to whether the local factories that come into the scheme will be expected to place all their resources at the Company's disposal, Mr. Payne replied in the negative. "There will be no interference with their conduct of their business," he said. "No doubt they will retain certain portions of their accommodation for the continuation of their ordinary business, so they may keep their connections together." It is obvious that it would not be to Wycombe's future advantage that its position, as a high-class furniture centre should be endangered. There are, as pointed out by Mr. Healey (who was also at the interview), some classes of operatives, such as the polishers, whose particular craft will not be required in the manufacture of aeroplane parts.

For these the continuance of the ordinary branches of manufacture will provide employment.

In *"Flight"* magazine of 11th October 1917, the registration of the firm is recorded, with capital of £5,000 in £1 shares. Directors were noted as G. H. Thomas, H. Burrows and G. A. Peck.

With all the planning and enthusiasm initially shown, the completion of the new factory was justifiably expected in a few months yet it was to prove more protracted. One event that was arranged to hold the interest of the local people was a grand flying display. On the afternoon of Saturday 20th April 1918 a demonstration had been organised by Mr. F. H. Payne, the Managing Director of Wycombe Aircraft Constructors Ltd., to show off to the town the aircraft that so many had been working on and give a demonstration of its abilities. The visiting aircraft, a DH 9, was flown by well known aviator, Captain B. C. Hucks. He had been the first Englishman to loop the loop. Though the weather was not at its best, on his arrival over the town he gave a stirring flying display, after which he landed the aircraft at Abbey Barn Park.

The visit by Captain Hucks, R.A.F. had been arranged by Mr. Holt Thomas. Captain de Havilland had also hoped to fly from Hendon to take part in the display, but was unable to attend due to other more pressing commitments. During the afternoon other ascents were made to further demonstrate the aeroplane's capabilities. On the

A GRAND FLYING DISPLAY ARRANGED TO TAKE PLACE AT ABBEY BARN PARK,
20th APRIL 1918.
This newly developed aeroplane, the DH 9, was flown to Wycombe to demonstrate its ability and give workers in the town a chance to see the result of their work.

Photo - BFP.

first of these the Mayor of High Wycombe, Mr. O. Haines accompanied Captain Hucks. Mr. H. J. Cox accompanied him on the second, during which a series of manoeuvres were performed, including side slipping, looping the loop, and a thrilling spinning nose dive from about 3,000 feet.

CAPTAIN B. C. HUCKS.

Time was also allowed so the spectators could examine the aircraft at close quarters, to appreciate more closely the workings of this aircraft, it being one of the latest type to go into service. It was fully equipped for service with two machine guns, one at the front operated by the pilot, the other at the rear operated by the rear gunner.

During 1917 and into 1918 work on the site for Wycombe Aircraft Constructors factory proceeded. In the B.F.P. of 15th February 1918, we read, the contractors, the Wilfey Company Ltd., of London E.C., are making rapid progress with the project, at the time employing between 60 and 70 workmen to level the site. April, May and June articles in the local paper seem to indicate some problems with the workforce on this site, of which a great number were Italian. Whether or not this caused some dispute is unknown, but a complaint was made to the company indicating that more local men should be employed. This was rejected by the contractors, when they stated they would gladly employ far more men if they could get them; at the time they were wanting 100 more for at least four to five months work. Great efforts were made to bring the scheme to fruition. Shortages of materials created by war conditions

were no doubt having a serious effect on all schedules. The few months originally expected to complete the building soon passed.

A Company Secretary, Mr. T. Kemp-Walton, a General Manager, Mr. T. E. Payne, and several key men had been appointed. However, it was not until October 1918 that the factory reached the stage where they were in a position to start manufacturing. An advert found in the Bucks Free Press on 18th October implies that they were at last ready to take on the workforce to proceed with aircraft production. In the *Flight* magazine, 31st October, we find a reference to a very successful whist drive and dance held at the Town Hall in High Wycombe on 13th October for the staff and employees, which may have been to celebrate the start of production at the new firm. This great effort, though, was to come to nothing. Before a single aircraft could be completed, on 11th November 1918 the war came to an end. Inevitably, all military aircraft orders were cancelled soon after.

In the B.F.P. of 12th September 1919, a report stated that all aircraft work in the town would cease and it was hoped that they would all return to furniture manufacturing.

The site where "The Wycombe Aircraft Constructors" factory stood is clearly defined in the B.F.P. of 15th February 1918 where it states that the site, twenty-two acres in extent, formed part of the Bell Field allotment gardens extending from the Hughenden Avenue end of the gardens to the nearby roadway (Bellfield Road), by the Temple Chair Works and included the space by the side of the watercress beds, fed by the Hughenden Park Springs. Today the stream that fed those beds still runs by the footpath that travels from Hughenden Park out to Bellfield Road. The site lies on the other side of the footpath and at present is still occupied by the factory that was Broom and Wade. A part of that complex was the Wycombe Aircraft Constructors factory.

Further information by H. S. Broom, in his book, *"A Recorded History of CompAir Broom Wade,"* on page 14 states, – "H. S. Broom turned his attention to a building at Bellfield which had been used for the manufacture of aircraft. He paid £25,000 for the disused factory and an acre or two of land." So the factory that was built initially to produce aircraft during First World War, eventually became the site for the firm of "Broom and Wade" who became world renowned for their air compressors. In the Second World War, tanks were produced here. The road (Hughenden Avenue), as it rises up the hill, was originally built as a track for testing the tanks.

WORKERS FROM A LOCAL FIRM POSING TOGETHER WITH ONE OF THEIR PRODUCTS.

Photo – High Wycombe Library.

PROPELLER MANUFACTURING IN HIGH WYCOMBE 1914-1918

Unfortunately little has come to light about the town's involvement in propeller making during 1914/18. This was very skilled and exacting work. There is a reference to production at Clapton's Mill or the Wire Mill in Wooburn Green.

During the war Gommes took over another factory less than 100 yards from their main works in Leigh Street that had frontage onto the Desborough Road and here they produced propellers for the Integral Propeller Co. This was another part of the Holt Thomas organisation, set up initially in Kentish Town, London, to produce under licence 'Chauviere' (French) airscrews. It moved to the premises of what had been the British Deperdussin works at 16, Elthorpe Road in Upper Holloway during April 1914. This was to provide better working conditions that were urgently needed.

TWO OTHER FIRMS THAT WERE INVOLVED IN AIRCRAFT PRODUCTION

Both of these firms entered into aircraft production rather late in the war, but are worth a mention as they were involved with well known aircraft manufacturers.

The Davidson Aviation Co. Limited, in Grafton Street, High Wycombe, were making parts for the Royal Aircraft Factory SE5a. Some aircraft drawings belonging to this company were still in existence until a few years ago. On the 7th July 1919, some of the directors formed a new company, Davidson Motor and Carriage Co. Ltd. to take over the interests of Davidson Aviation Co. Ltd. Presumably the aviation business became a motor vehicle business.

The Croydon Aviation & Engineering Co. Ltd. acquired two Wycombe factories in 1917, those of Messrs. Birch and Cox, Queens Road, and Cecil Smith, Desborough Road. In February 1919 the firm was renamed "The Croydon Aviation and Manufacturing Co. Ltd.". They had a contract to produce spares for Martinsyde aircraft and were described as manufactures and dealers in aircraft. All the Directors, J. T. Cox, J. C. Smith, F. Lynch and H. J. de Courcy Moore, had Wycombe addresses at that time.

THE END OF THE WAR

The eleventh hour of the eleventh day of the eleventh month, 11am. on 11th November 1918, at last the war was over. A war of death and destruction on a scale that had never been experienced before. The consequences would still be felt for many years to come. For many, the war bought death and injury, to others ruin, yet some had managed to make fortunes from it, including some of those who had been providing the armaments, especially the new tools of war which must include the newly-evolved tank and the aeroplane. In Wycombe though, most of the furniture industry were only too glad to get back to what they knew best, to return to its chair-making. The furniture bosses were soon back in control; most of them had not really found great profit from their involvement in aircraft work and had not enjoyed working to such exacting requirements, set by an industry that always demanded the highest standards.

It must be said that it is greatly to their credit that the workers had achieved the standard of workmanship required. They also probably had their first taste of real mass production. The brains behind aircraft design had recognised the benefits of this method of production and had designed for it, breaking the product down into small, easily handled parts. The individual parts were then being produced in large quantities. There is reference to Holt Thomas having studied the mass production methods used on the German airships before the First World War.

Even though an example of mass production like this had been demonstrated in our own factories in High Wycombe, it would be many years yet before designs to take advantage of mass production methods would be considered in the furniture industry. It still remained an industry where quality depended very much on the skill of those individual craftsmen.

What happened to the men who had led the aircraft industry during the war years? Some, it would seem, very soon faded into obscurity, for after the war the surplus of aircraft from the R.A.F. was so great that it was many years before the development of new aircraft seemed viable. Some did struggle on, eventually to develop our aircraft industry and become leaders in their field.

*SEE APPENDIX 2, for a list of adverts in the BFP requiring aircraft workers for many of the factories in High Wycombe.

CHAPTER 3

1918 –1939. BETWEEN THE WARS

At the conclusion of the First World War, the huge demand for military equipment ceased. With the great surplus of aircraft and the cancellation of most military contracts, things began to look very bleak within the aircraft industry. It was to become an uphill struggle to develop and sell new aircraft within this greatly reduced market. Many ex-military aircraft were easily and cheaply converted for civilian use as passenger, mail and cargo carriers. Utilising this stock, the first small airlines emerged.

Holt Thomas continued to be involved in one such company, "Air Transport and Travel Ltd." which he had started as a subsidiary of Airco in October 1916 (such was this man's foresight and confidence). It was not surprisingly one of the first to start trading after the war. But with the changing situation he sold Airco to the "British Small Arms Co Ltd." (B.S.A.) in 1920. The cancellation of military orders at the end of the war and the total failure of other envisaged sales and endeavours had forced him to relinquish his hold on the firm. It was finally closed down in 1922, as B.S.A. had never really been interested in aircraft production. Air Transport & Travel was eventually to be merged into the leading British airline of the time, Imperial Airways. Holt Thomas's interest in aviation seems to have evaporated at this time and his efforts were from then on centred on raising a prize-winning herd of Friesian cattle whilst living at North Dean.

Airco had been turning out thirty aircraft a day, every day, by the end of the war. It had a work force of over 4,400 and was proudly advertised in *"Jane's All the World's Aircraft"* as the largest aircraft enterprise in the world. So came to an end the firm that had provided almost one third of the total aircraft produced (55,000) for the allied forces. Yet for all this, unfortunately Holt Thomas remains virtually unknown and certainly uncelebrated in any real way. Here was a man of great determination and foresight and today his achievements can be recognised as quite outstanding amongst those who sought to promote the aviation industry during those early and difficult years.

At the time of the sale of Airco, Geoffrey de Havilland, who had been employed there for thepast six years, decided to form his own company, and continue with aircraft manufacturing. With a group of personnel chosen from the Airco staff, (including Wilfred Nixon, Francis St. Barbe, Charles Walker and Frank Hearle), and a very generous £10,000 financial support from George Holt Thomas (considering the financial climate at the time), he proceeded to form a new company. On the 25th September 1920 the "de Havilland Aircraft Co. Ltd." came into being.

Following the First World War, those who decided to continue with the aviation industry certainly had to struggle to create a market. It was a time that was to bring to the front those people who would become the very heart of our future aircraft industry. In Wycombe there is little evidence of any involvement other than the occasional DH Moth wing spars and inter-plane struts being made during times when furniture work was slack. Generally, Wycombe's furniture industry soon settled back into its normal work. Wycombe Aircraft Constructors, for whom there had been such great hopes, came to nothing. The newly constructed factory may have been used for a time as a waste wood conversion mill, where wood waste was ground into something known as wood flour and used to make linoleum floor covering. By 1928 it had become derelict and Broom and Wade purchased the building and site to expand their business, which until then had been situated in Lindsay Avenue. Eventually it became one of the town's major employers and world-renowned for its air compressors.

During the 1920s we see the emergence of a type of flyer who would today be more often associated with the film industry, usually known as 'barnstormers'. Many would have been wartime pilots who hoped to make a living doing exhibition flying at events around the country (some doing 'crazy flying' cavorting around the sky in most extraordinary and dangerous ways). Some offered short pleasure trips for those brave enough to accept. In truth most of those involved found little financial reward in this occupation

The experience of one such man, William George Chapman, is worth mentioning. In 1949 after a lifetime in transport and aircraft engineering he retired locally to the village of Speen. Early in his working life he had been a keen cyclist and had worked in the cycle manufacturing trade and won many trophies and medals as a racing cyclist.

He moved onto motor transport prior to the First World War, and from 1920 until 1922, he operated an aircraft charter and joy riding company known as 'Leatherhead Aviation Services' from a base at Byhurst Farm, Chessington. Within this period he visited the Wycombe area and operated his aircraft from "the top of Marlow Hill" and at Beaconsfield, giving exhibitions and joy rides in his Avro 504K, G-EBAV. Prior to the First World War he had been amongst those pioneer flyers, at the time owning and flying one of the early 28 h.p. Deperdussin aeroplanes. After the war, in 1919, he bought a surplus DH 6 aircraft G-EANU for his own pleasure. He also bought two more Avro 504Ks, listed as G-EAHL and G-EBCQ.

The aviation business was run in conjunction with his already established automobile and omnibus concern. Unfortunately the whole business folded soon after a crash at Slough on the 20th August 1922, in which he was a passenger. The aircraft, G-EBAV, having completed a loop followed by an Immelman turn, went into a spin and nose-dived into a tree. All three occupants were injured and needed hospital attention. Although he continued working in the aircraft industry after this, he commented that "it had then been earning other people's fortunes".

Apparently the misadventure and his injuries had been responsible for bringing his business to an end. Reminiscing on this period in his life at a much later date he commented: "I had almost forgotten it all and I can tell you I often wish I had nothing to do with it." His daughter, Edith Grace, née Chapman, kept a photograph of her father in the 28hp. Deperdussin aircraft which was taken sometime during 1913/14.

AMY JOHNSON

July 1st 1903 - January 5th 1941

Amy Johnson, the famous aviatrix, captured the imagination of the world when in May 1930 she successfully flew solo from England to Australia. Remarkably, this was achieved in a second-hand de Havilland Gipsy Moth, G-AAAH, that she had christened "Jason". (The aircraft is now displayed in the London Science Museum.) In recognition of this flight, Amy was made a Fellow of the Royal Geographical Society.

AMY JOHNSON

IN THIS PHOTOGRAPH MR. WILLIAM CHAPMAN SITS IN HIS DEPERDUSSIN AIRCRAFT.
Members of his family stand behind him, from L to R - his wife, his children in front, Joe, Ann, Billy, and Edith Chapman. Behind them stand Mr. Chapman's parents who lived in Whitehouse Lane, Wooburn. On the left is Mr. Chapman's engineer, a Mr. Rollason, who was later believed to have formed his own company.

Photo Mrs. J.Coles.

She loved the Chilterns area, living briefly at Haddenham in 1937, during which time she took up gliding with the London Gliding Club at Dunstable. Later, moving to Princes Risborough, she rented an early Tudor house called "Monks Straithe", in Church Lane. Originally it was the vicarage to the church of St Mary's, situated opposite. It now has a plaque attached to the chimney in memory of its famous one-time resident.

Living nearby with his family, at Chestnut Farm House, Monks Risborough, was a Walter Edmund Fletcher, at that time a young naval officer of some note having been made a Fellow of the Royal Geographical Society for his part in the 1934 Polar Expedition. This mission had set out to find the North West Passage, a rumoured sea route from the Atlantic to the Pacific Ocean via the northern extremities of the North American (Canadian) landmass. Was it a myth or a fact? The Expedition discovered the route, but found it was only possible to navigate for a very short summer period before it quickly froze over again. They made several other important discoveries during the expedition. It was probably through this shared interest that Amy and he became acquainted. It would be a strange twist of fate that would cause their paths to cross again.

MONKS STRAITHE, CHURCH LANE, PRINCES RISBOROUGH. AMY JOHNSON RESIDED HERE IN THE LATE THIRTIES.

Photo – I.C.S.

Amy's love of speed was never more apparent than when she sat behind the wheel of her car. She was often seen around the area driving her car at great speed. On one such occasion she was fined for speeding in High Wycombe.

During the Second World War she joined that valiant band of flyers, the Air Transport Auxiliary (A.T.A.). Their job was to ferry military aircraft of almost any type to and from almost anywhere, relieving service personnel for more important tasks. Some of these pilots were women who had learnt to fly prior to the outbreak of war. Can you imagine the surprise, seeing a petite young woman in flying overalls alighting from a Lancaster bomber, having just ferried it from the manufacturers or a repair unit, to bring it in for squadron use. Such was their work. The usual reaction was to wonder where the pilot was, not being able to comprehend that a woman could possibly handle such an aircraft. In total over 300,000 aircraft were ferried by the A.T.A. pilots during the Second World War.

Two of her long standing family friends, John Hofer and his wife Alice, were living at "North Croft", in Wooburn Green (then situated on what is now the North Croft Estate). Learning that Amy was now with the A.T.A. at Hatfield, the Hofers invited her to stay with them. This she happily accepted, as it would allow her to move from the communal lodgings near the airfield. The only disadvantage was the journey, thirty miles by car every morning. Even this was made easier when arrangements were made for her to use an aircraft from White Waltham (only a few miles away and the headquarters of A.T.A.), to travel to Hatfield and back again each day.

The Hofers were owners of a small local engineering firm at Wooburn Green, "Screw Machine Products", in which Amy was a shareholder.

Her last flight somehow ended in tragedy, which has never been fully explained. Her aircraft, an Airspeed Oxford, came down in the Thames estuary. Some theories seem to imply she could have run out of fuel, others that she was lost and probably had to descend through cloud to get her bearings and could have been shot down by friendly fire. There have been claims to substantiate this.

Sadly, she would not be the only person to die in this tragedy. At the time a certain naval officer, having observed an aircraft (later confirmed as an Airspeed Oxford) ditch into the Thames estuary not far from his ship, saw what he thought was someone in the icy cold water and dived in to attempt a rescue. This courageous action sadly cost him his life. He was dragged onto another rescue vessel already unconscious and suffering from hypothermia from which he never recovered. The officer, Lieutenant Commander Walter Edmund Fletcher, was Captain of the vessel H.M.S. Haslemere. Was it Amy Johnson that he had seen and tried to save? Will we ever know?

Sunday, exactly one week later, Amy's parents, Will and Ciss Johnson, who had travelled with Betty, Amy's younger sister, to "North Croft", stood together with John and Alice Hofer and a friend of the Hofers, Mrs. McClaren. They raised their glasses to pay tribute to the memory of Amy, after which the glasses were washed, dried, then smashed, in the old traditional way.

On Tuesday the 14th January 1941, a memorial service was held at St. Martins in the Field. Tributes poured in from around the world, and all sections of the national press carried articles mourning the loss of this famous aviator.

"*Amy Johnson, Enigma In The Sky*", a biography by David Luff, is a very well-detailed book about her life.

THE 1930s

THE FLYING CIRCUSES COME TO TOWN

Many entrepreneurs were to make determined efforts during the 1930s to stimulate interest in flying. They were convinced there was a great future ahead for the whole industry, as a faster means of transport for both people and goods. The public still considered flying as at least an adventurous if not a hazardous occupation.

One of the new promotional ideas was the flying circus. These gave demonstrations and pleasure flights to all those interested. They travelled from town to town throughout England, Scotland and Wales. A pioneer of the concept was Alan Cobham.

Cobham's aviation career was launched in 1919/1920 when, with the Berkshire Aviation Company, he toured the country giving joy rides in a war surplus Avro 504K. He joined Airco at Hendon and gained valuable experience as an aerial photographic pilot. This was only a temporary situation, as Airco were soon to close down. Fortunately, Geoffrey de Havilland engaged him at the beginning of 1921 as the first pilot for his newly formed de Havilland Aeroplane Hire Service. Over the next few years he was rarely out of the cockpit, flying on newspaper assignments, routine photographic work, air taxi and charter flying that took him

throughout Europe and the Middle East. His duties included test flying of new types and entering them in performance competitions, winning the 1924 King's Cup Air Race flying the prototype DH 50.

On leaving the de Havilland Company in 1927, he founded his firm, Alan Cobham Aviation Ltd. Cobham's aim was primarily to stimulate a nation-wide interest in aviation, and to promote this by way of a touring air show. To see an aeroplane at close quarters was still a thrilling experience and to have a chance to fly in one, even better. Each major town would have its own special air day and so the National Aviation Day (later Display) was formed in 1931. Some 200 people were employed, along with 24 aeroplanes and 50 transport vehicles to tend the travelling circus. Aeroplane types used for the display included: -

Airspeed A.S.4 Ferry, Handley Page W.10 (one of these, G-EBMR, unfortunately crashed at Aston Clinton, Nr. Aylesbury, killing four crew members), Handley Page Clive, Avro 504, Avro Cadet, DH 82A Tiger Moth, DH 83 Fox Moth, Desoutter, Spartan Mk 11, Cierva C 19 Autogiro and a Rhonbussard Glider.

Wycombe was not to miss out on these events. Visits by the Cobham Flying Circus were made in May of 1932 and 1933, June 1934 and July 1935, with reports of each year's event being reported in the Bucks Free Press (BFP).

As Sir Alan, Cobham would later be better known for his work pioneering in-flight refuelling systems, with his company, Flight Refuelling Company Ltd. Today this business still exists at Bournemouth International Airport.

THE BRITISH HOSPITALS AIR PAGEANT (BHAP)

Another group of enthusiastic aviators formed the British Hospitals Air Pageant (BHAP) in 1933. Organised by Jimmy King, it included fifteen pilots and three parachutists, among them several well-known record holders from the aviation world. Their Director, C. W. A. Scott, explaining the object of the tour, said, "*It is my intention to give a hospital, at each town in our itinerary, a substantial cheque on the conclusion of our visit.*" The object of the tour was to raise at least £20,000 a year, for five years, to hand over to British Hospitals. At each event the local hospital would receive ten percent of the gross gate receipts, £30 worth of flying tickets, usually used as prizes in locally organised events and one third of the programme sales. "*Apart from the financial benefit Hospitals will receive by this extensive tour, I feel sure the Air Displays will do much to demonstrate the value of aircraft and stimulate a wider and greater interest in the development of Civil Aviation, an important factor in the future prosperity of the Empire."*

Pilots, aircraft and engineers gathered at Ford Aerodrome in Sussex that year, where they were equipped with special uniforms of dark jackets and light trousers. Colonel James C. Fitzmaurice was to compère the shows. He had made a name for himself as Commandant of the Irish Air Corps and by flying the Atlantic East to West in 1926. Their aircraft included the popular Avro 504K flown by E. W. 'Jordie' Jordan and featured, as part of their demonstration, the wing-walker Harry Willis. This was real wing-walking, not strapped into a metal frame, but standing up on

SIR ALAN COBHAM'S FLYING CIRCUS – HIGH WYCOMBE 1932

Cobham's flying circus first came to Wycombe on Wednesday 27th May 1932. Operating from a site at the top of Marlow Hill, then known as Whincups Field (where the Girls' High School now stands), flying continued there well into the evening.

As we scan the preceding week's editions, we find once more the Bucks Free Press giving us all the up to the minute information on the forthcoming events and one can imagine the air of anticipation developing as the event drew closer.

Competitions for the free flights were organised and the winners announced as the day

FLYING INTO HIGH WYCOMBE AND OVER TOTTERIDGE ROAD, a formation from Alan Cobham's flying circus, comprising an Avro 504N, a Puss Moth and a Monospar ST12. Their destination, Whincups Field, is in the mist at the top left corner.

Photo - Ronald Goodearl

the top wing of the biplane and waving to the crowd as they swooped low in front of the crowds, with just a rope to hold onto. Another was the bizarrely decorated B.A.C. Planette, a powered glider, which was painted like a fish by the well-known artist, Heath Robinson, today well remembered for his unorthodox designs and inventions. The largest aircraft with the group was a DH84 Dragon, provided by W.A. Rollason Ltd.

drew near. Civic dinners were arranged to entertain the pilots and organisers, and many local dignitaries found themselves offered a chance to be hauled aloft in one of the participating aircraft. The BFP of Friday 3rd June 1932 gives a detailed report in the County Gossip column of the display held on the 27th May under a title of 'People becoming air-minded'. The reporter himself had also obviously enjoyed an air experience as related here –

AN AERIAL VIEW OF HIGH WYCOMBE

The view of High Wycombe from an aeroplane must have given satisfaction to the City Fathers who availed themselves of Sir Alan Cobham's invitation to fly during the air pageant on Friday. Airmen will pass over this part of Bucks without realising there is a factory town below them. Surrounded by beautifully wooded hills the valley presents a panorama of colour, seen now at its best with foliage in full leaf. There are many lovely gardens, which the passer by does not see. You see High Wycombe in perfection from the clouds. From an altitude each garden plot and open space represents a spot of colour in a beautiful mosaic pattern.

A six-minute flight in the airliner took in an area of about twenty miles. It only gave time for a passing glimpse of other people's gardens and the villas beside them; a perfect pattern of planning and architecture, at least, so it seemed to the eye, one thousand feet above.

WATCHING A FILM

There was no more sensation, once the airliner had ceased to sway as it left terra firma, than is felt watching a moving picture presenting an aerial view. You look out on a massive wing of the liner, which suggests a huge bird flying over the town of pigmies; gliding along through space with all sense of speed forgotten. Before the liner began to climb it seemed to be licking the hedges and skimming the treetops. West Wycombe Road where "ribbon development" is complained of, looked like a little baby ribbon; that black line was the railway to Princes Risborough.

The sense of location became more difficult. We had gradually turned until we were towering at high altitude above Amersham Hill and Totteridge. The Grammar School was a definite landmark. Again we seem to be engaged in a hurdle race over hedges and hillocks, without feeling any motion. There was the "lift" feeling once, when we lost altitude, and the next thing we were watching a few "beetles" crawling along the London Road – actually cars doing probably forty miles an hour. We had a good view of Wycombe Abbey School, and in a few seconds had reached earth again and were taxiing along the ground.

THE YOUNG IDEA

Parents who were too timid to fly themselves stood by and saw their boys and girls dashing through the enclosure to be ready for the next flight. It will not take many years for the younger generation to realise that bicycles and motor cycles are commonplace; they will be eager to fly and will fly. We were talking to a gentleman who was in the R.A.F. during the war and took part in bombing expeditions. In a technical way he described the risks they had to take, the comparatively poor types of machine then used and the improvements which had been brought about in twelve years. During the demonstration at High Wycombe we came to the conclusion that ladies were more eager to fly than men. The weather conditions were not ideal and many flights were made in a downpour of rain; the droning of the aeroplanes was heard throughout the day until a late hour.

WEATHER REPORTS

Aviators receive special reports of weather conditions from the Air Ministry. Sir Alan Cobham had the best report for three months for High Wycombe on Friday! Yet the actual conditions could not have been very much worse, although there was no high wind. Our methods of forecasting meteorological conditions do not prove we have mastered this science. Amateurs in this country are more successful in foretelling weather conditions than the weather office. They may be good at guessing. The Beaconsfield weather prophet has never believed that the summer was going to be a success, and so far we have had no cause to dispute his forecast.

EVOLUTION IN SPEED

The majority of people do not believe in "safety first," says Sir Alan Cobham. Among young people, at any rate, there is no desire to shirk an element of risk; and this, the mastery of the air has involved. Sir Alan stresses the fact that people do not require any special mentality to become successful in aviation, in fact he declares that the heroes of long distance flights are not more than normally intelligent. Motor cyclists will become aviators. We recall a conversation in the early days of 1913, with B. C. Hucks, one of the first to win fame as a flying man. He said that flying attracted him because he wanted a greater sensation of speed than he could get out of his motor bike. He was sure commercial flying would come, but the immediate use he saw for flying was "in the event of war, aeroplanes would be the eyes of the army."

The year 1914 proved his words. Today Sir Alan Cobham urges that flying can be the greatest factor in the cause for peace. "When there is constant flying between countries we shall break down fossilised ideas and get to know each other better."

SIR ALAN COBHAM'S FLYING CIRCUS – HIGH WYCOMBE 1933

The Bucks Free Press carried the following reports of the Flying Circus in May 1933, entering into the spirit of the show by running a competition that offered prizes to those able to guess the height of an aircraft as it travelled over High Wycombe. The winners were all to be awarded free flights.

Edition of Friday 5th May 1933

Sir Alan Cobham is to visit Marlow Hill, High Wycombe, on Wednesday May 17th. The Bucks Free Press has arranged for twelve free flights in one of his airliners. Readers are advised to keep their eyes on the skies on Tuesday, May 9th. At about 6.15 p.m., a mystery plane will fly over High Wycombe, emitting a trail of smoke. Free flights will be awarded to twelve competitors who estimate most correctly, the height of the aeroplane at the time it emits smoke. The arrival of the mystery plane will be announced by the roar of its 500hp. Siddeley engine. Before releasing the smoke signal, the pilot will give a thrilling display of looping, rolling and diving, as a foretaste of the great spectacle of the "Air Circus" the following week.

A coupon printed below the item was to be used to enter the competition.

Edition of Friday 12th May stated: -

The pilot, Mr. R. W. Ogden advised that "he had carried out a flight over the town in connection with the Bucks Free Press Height Judging Competition at a height of 862 feet."

This was followed by the list of the winning entries-

Mr W.G. Gomm, 41, Westbourne Street. (864 ft.) Mr. J. Taylor, Flint Cottage, Oakridge Road. (885 ft.) Mr. Harry Church, Lacey Green. (872 ft.) Mrs. E.A. Hole, 137, Gordon Road. (873 ft.) Mr. A.W. Cousens, 27, Coningsby Road. (873 ft.) Mr. W.T. Pond, 13, Marlow Road, Marlow. (850 ft.) Mr. William Match, 24, Victoria Street. (850 ft.) Mr. J. Hartley, 80, Eaton Avenue. (850 ft.)

Mr. Sydney Mellers, 8, Lucas Road. (850 ft.) Mr. S.G. Luker, 137, Dashwood Avenue. (850 ft.) Mr. L.R. Howland, 15, Terry Road. (875 ft.) Miss A. Price, 56, Temple End. (893 ft.)

Sir Alan Cobham will personally conduct and fly in the air display, his aim being to defeat the proposals made recently at Geneva to place civil aviation under the stranglehold of international control. Were this to happen, a flourishing industry would be doomed to stagnation. Gone would be the leadership won by the British aircraft industry, vanished would be the employment for thousands of skilled workers.

No opportunity of thrilling and instructing the public has been omitted from the programme of 20 events, which will be given twice daily at 2.15 pm. and 5.30 pm. The parachutist taking a header into space; a miniature Schneider Trophy Race within constant view of the spectators; a breathtaking display of aerobatics in formation and a humorous demonstration of "aerial pig sticking" will add to the excitement of the great display. Members of the public will have the opportunity of taking passenger flights in aircraft performing in certain events; as for example the impressive flypast and the parachute descent.

A sensational exhibition of really crazy flying, a demonstration of wing walking and a fearless display of upside down flying by a world famous pilot will be among the outstanding thrills of the programme. A display of trapeze aerobatics, at a height of 700ft., demonstrations of the Autogiro and other new types of aircraft, are amongst the notable attractions. Sir Alan's squadron is composed of such distinguished pilots as Flying Officer C. K. Turner-Hughes and Mr. C. W. H. Bebb, masters of the art of aerobatics, Flight Lieutenant A. H. C. Rawson, the famous pioneer test pilot of the Autogiro, Flight Lieutenant H. C. Johnson and Captain J. D. Parkinson, well known as pilots of Sir Alan's Handley Page and Airspeed Airliners, Messrs. Ivor Price and H. Ward, the leading parachutist, Mr. Martin Hearn, most fearless of wing walkers and the two redoubtable exponents of crazy flying, Captain A. N. Kingwill and Mr. W. MacKay, ("Dare devil Red MacKay.") Sir Alan has assembled the greatest gathering of air talent yet brought together in one organisation, for he is determined to stir everyone to give enthusiastic support to the cause of British aviation.

HIGH WYCOMBE 1933 – BRITISH HOSPITALS AIR PAGEANT

On Wednesday 14th June 1933 the BHAP visited Wycombe. Some fifteen pilots and three parachutists were included along with a remarkable collection of aeroplanes.

C. W. A. Scott, famous for his long-distance flights, winner of two major transcontinental air races and his recent record breaking flight from Australia to England in his DH60 Moth (VH-UQA, an Australian registration). A brand new DH 83 Fox Moth. Captain R. H. McIntosh, Captain Earl B. Fielden of Aviation Tours Ltd., William Rollason of Rollason Air Services, Lionel Anderson, John K. Morton – all pilots of fame in the thirties

AVRO 504K FLOWN BY E.W. 'JORDIE' JORDAN, WITH WING WALKER HARRY WILLIS, performing one of his famous feats during a British Hospitals Air Pageant that travelled the country, raising funds for local hospitals.

Photo - BFP.

A fascinating range of machines was assembled for the public's pleasure and education. Included was the only biplane ever built by Miles Aircraft of Reading, the Pobjoy "R" powered Miles Satyr, G-ABVG, painted in a very smart red and white chequer board scheme by its new owner, Mrs. Victor Bruce. Aerobatic demonstrations of the Satyr were normally flown by Flt. Lt. John Pugh. The converted Fairey Fox Bomber, G-ACAS, also came from Mrs. Bruce's company, Luxury Air Tours. Her event in the Pageant in this aeroplane was billed as the "Fox Dive". Two passengers would be given the ride of their lives by diving at 250 mph to within fifty feet of the ground! The Cornwall Aviation Company's Spartan Three Seater, G-ACAF, came and was flown by Captain Percival Phillips. The prototype twin Pobjoy "R" powered General Aircraft Monospar S.T.4, G-ABUZ, and a DH83 Fox Moth, the all yellow first production example, G-ABUP, came from Aviation Tours Ltd. They also provided Avro 504K G-EBYW, usually flown by E. W. "Jordie" Jordan, complete with wing walker Harry Willis.

The following report in the Bucks Free Press on 16th June 1933 under the title "Air Thrills at Wycombe Pageant" gives a very good insight into the reporter's experience as he viewed the aircraft and then after careful consideration took to the air.

AIR THRILLS AT WYCOMBE PAGEANT

HUNDREDS TAKE THEIR FIRST FLIGHT

In future I shall have a common feeling for the fly and even an affinity for the sparrow. I know what it feels like to walk along the ceiling. I have just taken my first flight. Last Wednesday the British Hospitals Air Pageant was held at High Wycombe. On Marlow Hill, a meadow had been converted into an aerodrome, where there were massed ranks of aircraft. I examined them with care. It was difficult what plane should have the honour of taking me for my first flight. Finally it was a toss up between the Gipsy Moth, in which Mr. Scott made his first record flights to and from Australia, the Fairey Fox, which dodders along at 200 miles an hour or the new Dragon Air Liner. At first I favoured the little contraption of Mr. Scott's, it would be something to make the boys down at the "Old Bull and Bush" turn green with envy. But finally I plunged for the airliner, feeling there was safety in numbers. Seven other nervous looking people climbed into the cabin with me.

Before I took to the air I had watched someone walking up and down the wings of an aeroplane in flight, with as much calm as if he had been walking down Wycombe High Street. It was reassuring. A mechanic swung the two propellers. The engines roared. I waved farewell to my wife and family. Suddenly I realised we were no longer on the ground and in fact were hovering over the parish church. We swung round to the west and I caught a glimpse of the big crowds at Loakes Park sports meeting. Then we steered a course above the straight white stretch of West Wycombe Road, until we circled higher and higher over West Wycombe Hill, which looked like a mere ant heap. On towards Bradenham and then we turned and I slowly watched the world come nearer and nearer. Was it to be a false landing? A farmyard flashed beneath. I saw a lady grinning at us benignly. Then we bumped down on the ground; it was the aerodrome again. We seemed to have travelled from Bradenham in a few seconds.

By this time, most people in Wycombe will have flown, but for the benefit of those who have not, allow me, a man who has flown in an aeroplane, to tell you that it's easy. Give me an aeroplane and I will fly to Paris, or even the Antipodes.

The pageant itself was full of thrills. I watched the wing walking expert sitting on the top plane of a machine that was flying at 90 miles an hour. Captain Phillips, the aerobatic expert, did a continuous series of loops and twists and rolls. Then passengers were invited to share with him the thrills of aerobatics. The announcer had difficulty at first, in persuading people to allow themselves to be turned upside down in mid-air, but later there was quite a stream of bold spirits, one of whom assured me that it was much more pleasant than it might appear.

A small aeroplane, described sometimes as a "motor cycle of the air", gave an exhibition of "crazy flying", showing how not to fly an aeroplane and emphasising the mistakes a new pilot is taught to avoid. The pilot showed the most breath taking skill, particularly when skimming over the meadows with the wings of the plane almost tipping the ground. The programme also included parachute descents, formation flying, air races and many other thrills.

Hundreds of people paid for joy flights, which could be taken for 4/- upwards. Most people were flying for the first time. They were offered a wide choice of craft, from the big airliner down to Scott's small record breaking Moth. The pageant served a double purpose, for it was not only the means of making a large number of people more "air-minded" but also produced funds for High Wycombe Hospital.

British Hospitals Air Pageants were being held that summer in about 200 of the principal towns of the country and it was hoped to raise at least £20,000 for British Hospitals. Several well-known aviators were taking part in the pageants,

including Charles W. Scott, the Hon. Mrs. Victor Bruce, Flt. Lt. Pugh, Captain Phillips and Captain MacIntosh, and on Wednesday, Wycombe folk were taken for joy rides by one or other of these air celebrities

SIR ALAN COBHAM'S FLYING CIRCUS – HIGH WYCOMBE 1934

Once again in the 1st June 1934 edition of the Bucks Free Press we find the forthcoming "National Air Day" event is well covered in its article.

Sir Alan Cobham has arranged to give a National Aviation Day display at High Wycombe on Tuesday 12th June. This year his team of twelve brilliant pilots with their varied fleet of fast new aircraft has set out to give one of the finest air displays ever seen.

Flight Lieutenant Geoffrey Tyson, who is undoubtedly Britain's finest aerobatic pilot, must be seen to be believed. The most hardened of thrill seekers will feel the suspense as he swoops down in a dive and whisks up a handkerchief from the ground with his wing. A display of aeroplane towed gliding and looping in a glider will be given by Miss Joan Meakin, the young English girl who recently made a towed flight in her glider from Germany to England. Another remarkable new exhibition is the radio-batic display. A Siddeley-Avro trainer is equipped with a wireless transmitter and during the wonderful demonstration of advanced aerobatics, the pilot will broadcast a description of his evolutions, his words being relayed by loudspeakers to the public.

A novel item is the "pull-off" parachute descent. This type of drop can be made safely from a low altitude, so the spectators may have a closer view of the operation of the parachute. Mr. Ivor Price, the leading British parachutist, has made over 300 jumps and will demonstrate both the "pull-off" and "delayed drop" descents. The programme of 16 events lasts three hours and is given in full during the afternoon from 2.30 and again during the evening from 6.15. It includes speed and height judging competitions, with free flights for the prize winners. Admission is 1s.3d for adults, 6d for children and 1s for cars. Flights are available from 4s.

In the Bucks Free Press article of 8th June 1934 the results of the recent ballot for free entry to the show on the 12th is given.

Following the postal ballot the following twelve have won free admission to the ground on Marlow Hill and a free flight in a Giant Airliner.

COBHAM'S HANDLEY PAGE CLIVE AT WHINCUPS MEADOW, HIGH WYCOMBE 12th JUNE 1934

Photo ARCHIBALD SMITH

Mr. F. Oxlade. 150, Totteridge Road. Master Maurice G. Bull. 57, Roberts Road. Mr. A. M. Samman. Fairfield, Bourne End. Mrs. A. Tapping. Lynton, Princes Risborough. Mr. Cyril Simpson. 2, Mead Street, Wycombe Marsh. Miss N. L. Matthews. Homeleigh, Lakes Lane, Beaconsfield. Miss Mollie E. King. 35, Amersham Hill. Mr. J. Hudson. Farnborough, Lower Road, Sands. Mr. G. A. Dean. Castlemorton, 4, Victoria Road, Marlow. Mr. O. C. Coles. Burnhams, Naphill. Mr. A. F. Smith. 36, Green Road, Terriers. Mrs. N. E. Newman. 30, Council Houses, Chalfont St. Giles.

Twelve aircraft will take part in a programme of sixteen events at each display. A feature will be a thrilling looping the loop exhibition by Flight Lieutenant Geoffrey Tyson, who will pass upside down through a hoop erected on the aerodrome, pick up a handkerchief from the ground with his wing tip and fly inverted at a height of only 50 feet. Captain W. Mackay, well known to the public as "Dare Devil Red MacKay", will give a new version of his hair raising crazy flying. Another thrilling spectacle will be the aerobatics display in formation by the team of expert pilots who have won fame as the "Three Aces".

FAMOUS GLIDER GIRL

Miss Joan Meakin, the famous young Germany to England glider pilot, will give an outstanding demonstration of aeroplane towed gliding and glider aerobatics with her "Rhonbussard" glider. She will be towed up to a height of 1500 feet behind an aeroplane and at

that height will disengage the towing cable. During her glide down to earth she will repeatedly loop the glider and show that normal aerobatics can be performed with ease. Miss Meakin was the first woman to loop a glider. Mr. Ivor Price, the leading British parachutist, who has made more than 550 drops, will demonstrate the "pull-off" method of parachuting from the wing of an aeroplane. Passengers in the airliner will watch at close range the whole process of the parachute unfolding itself and opening and see Mr. Price snatched from his platform and safely land on the ground. Mr. Price will also make a delayed drop from 2,000 feet, falling for several seconds before releasing his parachute.

WIRELESS

Wireless communication is a vital part of the organisation of an airway. In order to demonstrate the efficiency of radio-telephone equipped aircraft and aerodromes, a Siddeley-Avro trainer has been fitted with a transmitter, to enable the pilot to speak to the broadcast coach. His voice will be relayed to the spectators through the loudspeakers, and he will describe the evolution of his machine whilst carrying out a display of aerobatics and crazy flying. This event is also intended to demonstrate the right way and wrong way of controlling an aeroplane.

There will be aerobatic flights for passengers with Captain Phillips, D.F.C., who has a reputation for being unable to fly straight and level for more than ten seconds. Captain Phillips is now flying an up to date Siddeley-Avro trainer.

In the Bucks Free Press article 15th June 1934 the success of the Air Display is reviewed.

That High Wycombe is becoming more air minded was amply proved on Tuesday, when Sir Alan Cobham's National Aviation Day display thrilled crowds of both young and old – spectators and passengers – sometimes only a few feet above the "aerodrome" in Whincups field at the top of Marlow Hill. Dozens of people took their first flight, and it says for the confidence they gained that many went up a second time, choosing a smaller craft after the airliner.

It was noticeable too, that on the maiden trip faces were whiter than usual and lips pursed together, but muscles had relaxed and smiles were broad when the plane came to earth. A surprising number of children were passengers in the liners. This was a promising feature of the day, since it is the younger generation who need to lose fear of the air for the future. At a rough estimate it could be said too, that young women outnumbered the men passengers. It seemed that they were willing to dare more on stunt flights. It raises an interesting point, which may be explained when one thinks of the splendid example set by Mrs. Mollison and Miss Jean Batten.

SIR ALAN COBHAM'S CAMPAIGN

I spoke to Sir Alan on the question of air mindedness of England at the moment, writes a Bucks Free Press representative. "Do you consider," I asked him, "that England is backward compared with other countries?"

"Yes" he replied, "definitely, but in my travels I find it is being rapidly overcome. We are distinctly behind in the matter of airports. The question of provision of municipal aerodromes is vital and every town of importance, such as High Wycombe, should be urged to find a flying field."

"This can be done, with the help of an expert airman, by a process of elimination. Select a number of fields that seem to be suitable, and then gradually look for all the points that make a good, safe flying field, combing out bad fields until at least there remains only the best. Then concentrate on making the field and town widely known."

"Have you any idea of a suitable field in this district?"

"No, when I come I merely ask for a field. This field suits our purpose, but as a municipal aerodrome it would be unsuitable, since the average person might easily come to grief when taking off or landing on it".

During the day people gasped as they watched a plane diving to earth at 300 mph, or saw a plane flying in an inverted position as naturally as if it were the right way up. There was formation flying, parachute descent, aerobatics, the picking up of a handkerchief from the ground with the tip of a wing, a thrilling air race with local passengers and several humorous items which called for great skill on the part of the pilot.

SIR ALAN COBHAM'S FLYING CIRCUS – HIGH WYCOMBE 1935

AN ADVERT PLACED IN THE BUCKS FREE PRESS, FRIDAY 26th. JULY 1935.

NEXT WEDNESDAY
JULY 31st
SIR ALAN COBHAM'S
GREAT NEW
AIR DISPLAY
Britain's Finest Pilots in Flying's most Daring Feats!
20 NEW BRILLIANT EVENTS!
MARLOW HILL
HIGH WYCOMBE
Frequent Services of Buses pass the ground
Afternoon and Evening Displays, 2.30 and 6.30
Continuous 2.30 p.m. till dusk
Admission 1/3; Children 6d.; Cars 1/-; Cycles 2d.
FLIGHTS WITH FAMOUS PILOTS from 4/-

THE REPORT ABOUT THE EVENT APPEARED IN THE BUCKS FREE PRESS 2nd AUGUST 1935 UNDER THE TITLE:

AEROBATICS OVER WYCOMBE

High Wycombe resounded to the throbbing of mighty aero-engines on Wednesday, when Sir Alan Cobham's team of airmen paid a visit to the town. As on previous occasions, the large field at the top of Marlow Hill was chosen for the flying ground, above which a daring pilot did high-speed aerobatics in the azure sky. It was delightful to be borne aloft in those colourful dragonflies, the "Avro Cadets".

Hundreds of people from High Wycombe and the neighbourhood experienced for the first time that peculiar sense of lordliness, that superiority over the mundane things of earth, which an aeroplane flight can give. Perhaps the biggest thrill of the display this year was provided by Miss Naomi Heron-Maxwell, an amateur parachutist, whose breathtaking leaps into space proved that the parachute is a well tried invention which no one should hesitate to use, should the emergency arise.

During the evening, the planes, including an airliner and an autogyro, were busy carrying passengers on long and short flights. Flight Lieutenant Johnson, chief pilot, was in charge of the display. A number of members of the Town Council accepted invitations to take a flight, among them being Alderman W. E. Ellis, who is 82.

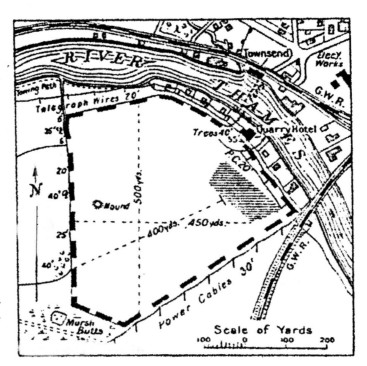

MAP OF LANDING GROUND AT COCK MARSH

AN AIRFIELD AT BOURNE END
1930s

Cock Marsh at Bourne End was used during the 'thirties as a landing ground for light aircraft visiting the Quarry Hotel. This was featured in *"Flying"* magazine of July 1933 in a series by the Automobile Association (who, at that time, also catered for aviators) about small air-strips available to "weekend flyers". Several photographs exist, showing visiting light aeroplanes. Amongst these is a visiting party, believed to have flown in from an international meeting at Heston in the early 'thirties.

Included in this party were DH60G Moth, G-AAAA (formerly owned by Geoffrey de Havilland), owned by Oliver Tapper of the Automobile Association. Others present were:- G-AAXJ, DH80A Puss Moth; G-ABBD DH60 X Moth; G-ABCE, Avro 616 Avian Sport; G-EBKB, Avro 504K; F-ALER, Farman 291; D-2475, Klemm L.26C.II and D-2854, Klemm L25D.VIIR.

Cock Marsh is described as "A Riverside Resort" at Bourne End in the Thames Valley and is classified as definitely "a place to go".

"The landing ground is not easy to find, but the loop in the river is unmistakable, and the railway running north from Maidenhead crosses it nearby. The landing ground would be better for some sign, such as a large and flamboyant 'Flying' windsock. There was no indicator and

the cattle, together with a small power line, which were both obvious features of the ground, would have raised doubts about any field less certainly marked by nature and the Great Western Railway.

The A.A. sketch map shows the power line, a mound and a possible soft spot, which are all obvious from the air and easily avoidable. We found the cattle quite well behaved also. Except for these items, the ground has an excellent smooth grass surface and is amply large. It is, in fact, better than many regular aerodromes.

Mr. S. G. Fletcher, the enterprising Secretary of the Quarry Hotel, is helpful and hospitable to a degree. His hostelry is clearly indicated, in more senses than one, to aviators and the aerial visitor can taxi up to within a yard of the garden gate. Cuisine and cellar, judged from all too brief samples, seem to be excellent.

The hotel stands in its own grounds, with a frontage on the river of 150 yards and the back wall, which is right on the aerodrome, bears the name of the house in letters large enough to read from the air at a reasonable distance. The approaches to the landing ground are not precisely flat, but present no difficulty, even to a "floater".

The landing fee of two shillings [10p], should be paid to Mr. Fletcher, who acts in the matter for the Odney Estate Ltd., the owners of the field who kindly permit its use as a landing ground. Mr. Fletcher admits to having a plan to build a lock-up in his garden, for the better peace of mind of overnight visitors, as Ranald Porteous was to find out later!

AIRCRAFT PARKED AT THE REAR OF THE QUARRY HOTEL
A popular spot on the Thames in the 1930s.

Photo - Brian Print.

This decidedly is a Bourne to which no traveller will fail to return and is, unlike most aerodromes, an End in itself."

"More Tales of the Fifties" by Peter G. Campbell, published by Cirrus Associates, has some memories recounted by Ranald Porteous (better known for his demonstrations at Farnborough in the late 'fifties/early 'sixties in an Auster aircraft). Some time in the 'thirties, Ranald borrowed a Kronfeld Drone (a glider with a Douglas twin-cylinder motorcycle engine) from an acquaintance at Hatfield, with the intention of visiting friends at Bourne End, where there was a small grass landing field just behind the Quarry Hotel. "This journey of some twenty-five miles was completed in just under an hour and the Drone was duly tethered down for the night before my host (an old rowing Blue) ferried me across the river. Next day we were horrified to find that cows, of whose presence I had been unaware, had chewed great lumps out of the Drone's tail. An engineer from White Waltham performed miracles and the Drone's owner was unexpectedly forgiving."

Today all that remains to indicate the site of the Quarry Hotel, which was burnt down in the late 'thirties, are the steps that lead up from the river to the popular little bar/restaurant called "The Bounty". It is just upstream of the railway bridge that still crosses the river here, as it did in the 'thirties.

NEW DEVELOPMENTS IN AIRCRAFT PLY

A local man, Mr. Andrew Oliver, was to play a very important role during the Second World War. He was the adopted son of Mr. Baker, owner of the Wycombe firm Walter Baker, who were the town's veneer and ply manufacturing specialists. In the 'thirties their claim to fame, as Andrew said, "came from the fact they had supplied some, much, or all of the veneer panel work used in fitting out the large ocean liners of the day." He was sent to Germany in the early 'thirties as part of his ongoing training in the industry, to study and gather information about the newly developed "Plastic Glues". This type of wood glue proved to be one of the strongest known and was eminently suitable for plywood production. Then, he had no idea how valuable this knowledge would be in the years to come.

Shortly after his return to England, he was able to offer advice on glues and ply to a potential customer who was interested in buying materials for building a new light aeroplane of French origin, called the "Mignet H.M.14 Pou du Ciel" or, as it became known in England, "The Flying Flea". Realising Andrew was well informed about the subject, the customer asked him if he would like to help with the construction during his spare time. The aircraft, mainly made of timber and ply, was a popular "home build" design of the 'thirties. Over 80 were built in England. Unfortunately the design was unstable during certain manoeuvres and this resulted in several deaths. Eventually a flying ban was imposed on the design.

With Andrew the experience of building this small aircraft would not be wasted. He had started to gain knowledge of aircraft structures whilst involved with the project. During the coming war this knowledge and experience would be invaluable.

By the 'thirties the aviation industry had learnt much from its earlier experience. Aircraft were slowly evolving and becoming accepted as a reliable form of transport, especially for the rich. Heroes and heroines of the air, as they were in the thirties, had made longer and longer flights, setting new records, showing that it was possible to make these journeys in some of the newest aircraft. Women certainly proved to be equal to men when setting some of the long distance records. Aerodromes were becoming established and facilitated easier travel to all corners of the Empire. The age of the flying boat, that needed no runway, landing on any stretch of convenient water, reached its peak during those years. The competitive spirit of the Schneider Trophy and other races had honed those participating to new levels of understanding in speed and streamlining. Slowly the biplane was to be replaced by the monoplane. Engines were far more powerful and reliable. Enclosed cabins offered far greater comfort. Some considered these years to be the golden years of flying, especially those who enjoyed the thrill of new unfettered adventure.

In the late 'thirties Barmoor Farm at Booker, located three miles south of High Wycombe, started to be developed, initially as a small landing strip for light aircraft. At the outbreak of the Second World War, it was taken over by the Royal Air Force, becoming R.A.F. Booker. Today it is Wycombe Air Park. (See Chapter 7.)

As the 'thirties drew to a close, those almost happy-go-lucky days were tainted with a new fear. Once again there were war clouds on the horizon. Germany was re-arming at an alarming rate, their army with Panzer fast attack divisions equipped with the new high speed Tiger tanks. Their air force (Luftwaffe) was being equipped with new aircraft and many of their pilots were being trained in flying schools in England, as under the Geneva Convention the training of military pilots was forbidden in Germany. Before arriving in England they would start training by learning to fly in gliders. The German Navy was building up a formidable fleet of new "pocket battleships", light, well-armed and fast, but still below the all-up weight limits set out by the League of Nations after the First World War.

The German Youth Organisation, a military based force, were being sent to England under the guise of educational visits and on their travels taking pictures and collecting information about our military bases. It would be during the war that information came to light that the so-called 'thirties "friendly visits" by their Zeppelin Airships were nothing more than photo-reconnaissance missions.

THE GRAF ZEPPELIN D-LZ127

It flew over Wycombe early one morning in the spring of 1939.

Photo- A. Ivermee

Looking back it would seem almost impossible not to know what was coming. Some people, well aware of the danger, tried to stir the government into action, but their words fell on deaf ears and for their trouble they were labelled warmongers. Prominent amongst these of course was Winston Churchill, who was only too aware of how inferior our own fighting forces had become. The British Prime Minister, Neville Chamberlain, tried to negotiate a treaty with Hitler for a lasting peace; this policy of appeasement was to fail miserably. He claimed that Hitler had deceived him. How could those politicians be so naïve, yet Russia too was persuaded that Hitler had no thoughts of territorial gains on their lands when he signed a treaty to prove this. Consequently their Western border was poorly defended, and it cost them very dear.

Germany soon started to intimidate other European countries. Hitler's intention was to retake the lands and colonies that had been stripped away from Germany after her First World War defeat. Here was a man who during his ranting had declared, "War is a certainty, there is no beginning or peace treaty."

There was no ambiguity, his intentions were clear. Firstly, on 15th March 1939 his army occupied part of Czechoslovakia. Chamberlain pledged support for Poland should their independence be threatened. Clearly if Britain went to war it was to be in response to Hitler's aggression. On 3rd September 1939, Hitler invaded Poland. Neville Chamberlain was forced to make the declaration, "We are now at war with Germany." But what could Britain do about the position in Poland? – Absolutely nothing.

In this country, but for the efforts of a few men, who had clearly recognised Hitler's intentions, who were driven by their overwhelming compulsion to do something, we could have been left with no up-to-date form of defence, certainly in the air. Only just in time the re-equipping of our squadrons with the new Hawker Hurricane and Supermarine Spitfire monoplane aircraft started to take their place as our main fighter defence aircraft, replacing the slower, outdated biplanes that had been considered the best type for the R.A.F. during the early 'thirties. We were facing the same fate as the rest of Europe.

In Poland one of their elite cavalry regiments bravely did the only thing they could to defend their country when invaded. With swords drawn they attempted to charge the German guns. They had no chance. Poland was overrun in days; they had nothing to halt the German advance. In Britain the question on every ones lips was, "Will we be next?" Many considered it inevitable

CHAPTER 4

1939 – 1945. THE SECOND WORLD WAR

After the declaration of war on the 3rd September 1939 everyone waited for the dreaded air attacks to begin, as seen in other European countries as a prelude to their invasion. Prime Minister Neville Chamberlain resigned, his policy of appeasement in tatters. Winston Churchill was invited to form a government. Wisely, and accepting the seriousness of the situation, he formed a coalition government, enabling him to choose those best suited to the task now facing them. An Expeditionary Force was sent to aid with the defence of France, as Hitler continued his advance across Europe. In Britain at first little happened: this period became known as "the phoney war". Those few months proved to be so vital, enabling Britain to start building defences strong enough to face the impending German offensive.

The inadequacy of the British fighting forces was immediately made evident when an Expeditionary Force was sent to France: it was overwhelmed by the superior German forces. Many small boats, in support of the Royal Navy, raced across the English Channel to rescue the remnant of that force trapped at Dunkirk, preventing the decimation of our army. Many were lucky to escape with their lives; but very little of their equipment was saved. France surrendered shortly after. Britain now stood alone, separated from war-torn Europe only by the English Channel. Most of the army's equipment, heavy guns and transport were abandoned; most of our aircraft sent there were destroyed. It would take considerable time to rebuild our forces. *Would there be time?*

Immediate Government action denied factories manufacturing non-essential goods any materials that were otherwise required for the war effort, which now took absolute priority.

This was a considerable blow to Wycombe's furniture industry, but some were already finding other work. Those quick to realise the seriousness of the situation started tendering for war work, producing items within their ability that would be required in our defence. Yet other factories that were less willing to change were almost at a standstill. This caused many men from Wycombe, who saw little prospect of continuing in their chosen profession (as in every other town in the country) to volunteer for the armed services. This soon changed when they were all bought under the control of the Ministry of Production – yes, they too were soon working long hours, seven days a week.

Very early in the war some became involved in the manufacture of aircraft components. By mid 1940, E. Gomme Ltd. was manufacturing complete wings and inter-plane struts for the de Havilland DH 82A Tiger Moth, a primary trainer for the RAF. At Woodley Aerodrome, near Reading, Phillips and Powis, who were manufacturing aircraft designed by F.G.Miles, also made use of Wycombe's skill base to assist in the production of parts for the Miles Magister primary trainer and the Miles Master advanced trainer. Risborough Furniture, Station Road, Princes Risborough, and the Hughenden Furniture Company, Slater Street, High Wycombe, were among these sub-contractors. Records show that production started at Risborough Furniture in December 1940. Here they produced wing ribs, centre section and wing spars, instrument and control panels, fuselage details, sub-assemblies and completely assembled wings, centre sections, tailplanes, fins and rudders. At Hughenden Furniture, production started in January 1941, producing fuselage details and completed assemblies of tailplanes, elevators, fins and rudders.

Between September 1940 and March 1941 approaches were made to High Wycombe's furniture industry. Once again they were to be involved in the manufacture of a new aeroplane. Harry Povey, Chief Production Engineer from de Havilland, accompanied by Lee Murray, the manager at their main works at Hatfield, spent some time in the town evaluating the furniture industry's capability to manufacture wooden components for this new project. They were encouraged when it became obvious that sufficient capacity and skill was still available within the town.

Later, members of the Furniture Manufacturers' Association were called to a meeting at Hatfield. They were soon enlightened as to the purpose of the meeting when Geoffrey de Havilland faced the members of the Association, and especially one man who he knew from previous working contact, with a simple question, "Well Mr. Heath, how about helping to build this Mosquito aircraft of ours?" Mr. Heath, owner of Heathland Furniture in Copyground Lane, High Wycombe, replied simply by stating, "Gentlemen, I will make you anything in wood, providing I get the backing of your drawing office." Wycombe's furniture companies were about to become some of the first sub-contractors helping to produce a remarkable new aeroplane. It was inevitable that Wycombe would be chosen, just as it was in the

First World War, then using its woodworking skills to help manufacture parts for the DH 4 and DH 9. This time, there was a difference – the expertise had become far more advanced.

THE DE HAVILLAND DH 98 MOSQUITO

What was it that was so special about this new aeroplane? Built as a private venture, the initial concept was of an unarmed bomber capable of out-flying contemporary fighter aircraft (as de Havilland had in the First World War, with the DH 4 and 9). At first those in authority viewed it with great scepticism. Built with a wooden structure (which many considered totally inappropriate), it proved to be both light and fast, capable of carrying a two thousand pound payload, equal to that expected of a medium bomber, whilst still capable of outpacing any of the opposing fighter aircraft. Once again Geoffrey de Havilland succeeded in producing a bomber aircraft which could rely on its speed for defence. The Mosquito became probably the most versatile British aircraft of the Second World War.

Sir Wilfred Freeman, who was responsible for development and production at the Air Ministry, had given his whole-heartedly support and backed the project against all the opposition. Another title given by those who knew of the involvement of the furniture industry was "Flying Furniture".

Even though initially unwanted by the Air Ministry, de Havilland's unique concept proved to be all they had initially intended and more. Forty-three variants of this design were developed during its working life, twenty-seven being significantly different. It became a very potent multi-role combat aircraft. Bomber Command's overall loss figures – Stirling 4.7 %, Halifax 3.3 %, Lancaster 2.9 %, the Mosquito only 0.5 % - emphasise the Mosquito's success in being able to carry out its task as intended and survive. With its wooden construction, the Mosquito probably had a radar signature of only 10% for an aeroplane this size, aiding its ability to enter enemy air space almost undetected. A study of official records shows varying maximum speeds quoted. One obtained while assessing the prototype at Boscombe Down gave 388 mph. at 22,000 ft (Merlin 21 engines).

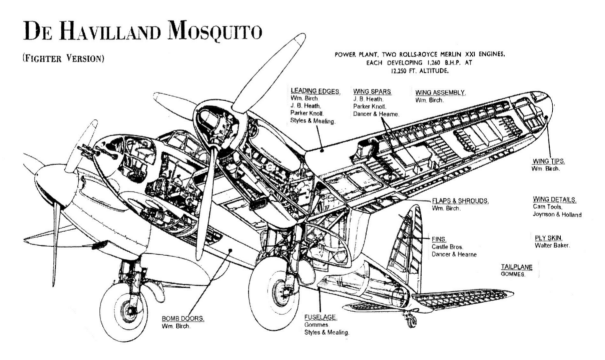

DE HAVILLAND MOSQUITO
(FIGHTER VERSION)

POWER PLANT, TWO ROLLS-ROYCE MERLIN XXI ENGINES, EACH DEVELOPING 1,260 B.H.P. AT 12,250 FT. ALTITUDE.

LEADING EDGES.
Wm. Birch.
J. B. Heath.
Parker Knoll.
Styles & Mealing.

WING SPARS.
J. B. Heath.
Parker Knoll.
Dancer & Hearne.

WING ASSEMBLY.
Wm. Birch.

WING TIPS.
Wm. Birch.

FLAPS & SHROUDS.
Wm. Birch.

WING DETAILS.
Cam Tools.
Joynson & Holland

FINS.
Castle Bros.
Dancer & Hearne.

PLY SKIN.
Walter Baker.

TAILPLANE
GOMMES.

BOMB DOORS.
Wm. Birch.

FUSELAGE.
Gommes
Styles & Mealing.

The Mosquito, known to most simply as the "Mossie", had several other names that reflect different attributes of this aeroplane. "The Wooden Wonder", which it most certainly was. "Termites Dream", gained from when first used in the Far East and it was discovered that the glue used, a "casein" cement (a milk derivative), was susceptible to attack by insects and fungus. On the production lines this was replaced with a new type of synthetic resin adhesive that proved far superior. Another was "Freeman's Folly", after Air Marshal

When matched against a Spitfire, both pilots agreed that the Mosquito was at least 20 mph. faster. Later development of the Rolls Royce engines helped it achieve a speed of 437 mph. at 29,000 ft. (Merlin 77 engines) in 1942. It remained the fastest combat aircraft in the world for another two and a half years.

Without doubt, this was our furniture industry's major contribution to the war effort. Whilst parts were manufactured elsewhere, High Wycombe firms manufactured wooden components for the entire airframe, these subsequently being taken for final assembly at de Havilland factories at Hatfield and Leavesden (near Watford). Probably the highest percentage of the wooden airframe components for Mosquitos built in England were produced in High Wycombe. Woods used in the construction were Sitka spruce, birch, balsa, ash, Douglas fir and walnut. An article written by Mr. J. B. Heath (owner of Heathland Furniture, one of the Wycombe firms involved), stated that they had produced parts for five thousand, five hundred and seventy aeroplanes. The total built, including those in Canada and Australia, was seven thousand, seven hundred and eighty-one.

High Wycombe was the acknowledged centre of the furniture industry in Great Britain. Its experience gained over the preceding years in the production of wood laminates and adhesives was greatly improved by the development of the new synthetic adhesives. It was this experience that bought them to the forefront when a choice of sub-contractors had to be made. Wood is a material of incomparable merits, but has some grave defects in its natural state, when used for structural members. Not a uniform and dependable material, like metal, its defects can be almost wholly overcome by the process of selection and lamination. Free from the fatigue and corrosion that occur in metal, it can also, if adequately protected, overcome the effects of degradation due to moisture and temperature.

The Mosquito was designed to be built in wood at a time when combat aircraft were designed and built in metal. The choice of wood offered major advantages. It was possible to reduce the initial design time and to build the prototype more rapidly than in metal. The use of wood avoided imposing additional strain upon metal supplies. Skilled labour was readily available, especially in High Wycombe, because of the restrictions imposed on furniture manufacturing.

The fuselage shell, a most outstanding structure, constructed in two halves on moulds, features a wood sandwich of ply / balsa / ply with local spruce reinforcement and stiffening at points where other components are attached. This helped to created a clean interior.

The wing is a single-piece construction, with main and rear spars and a stressed skin. The skin is reinforced by closely spaced span-wise stringers which, over the upper surface, are sandwiched between a double covering of skin, whilst the lower surface has a single skin. The wing spars are of box construction, manufactured mainly from laminated spruce booms with ply webs on both sides. The wing spars not only had to carry the aerodynamic loads, but also those imposed by the Rolls Royce Merlin engines and the undercarriage. Originally designed to carry a bomb load of two thousand pounds, this load was eventually doubled.

A very interesting and detailed description, *"Construction of the DH 98 Mosquito"*, is published and available from the de Havilland Heritage Centre at London Colney, Hertfordshire.

THOSE INVOLVED

Local companies identified as having manufactured wooden parts for the Mosquito include Dancer & Hearne, E. Gomme, Styles & Mealing, Heathland Furniture, Walter Bakers, Castle Brothers, William Birch, Cam Tools, Joynson & Holland and Frank Parker. It is probable that other Mosquito parts were manufactured locally by Plastalune (perspex canopies), High Duty Alloys (propellers, undercarriages and wheel hubs), F. Mealing (tubular steel engine mountings and exhaust stubs), and the Ministry of Aircraft Production factory in Coronation Road (undercarriage legs).

Fortunately today a very good collection of photographs that help to illustrate the town's contribution to the manufacture of the Mosquito have survived. Selected photos, complete with some details where known, are given in Chapter 5.

(To quote from the report of the 50th Anniversary Symposium held at British Aerospace, Hatfield, on the 24th November 1990, to commemorate the first flight of the aircraft in 1940, the Mosquito could be considered "Probably man's highest engineering achievement in timber".)

In High Wycombe one firm, that of Walter Baker, then an acknowledged leader in the production of plywood and veneer products, was soon involved in work requiring their expertise, producing much needed plywood panels and moulded ply sections. Because of his experience gained while in Germany prior to the war with the new synthetic adhesives, Andrew Oliver (the foster son of Mr. Walter Baker and by then the works manager) had become a leading authority in its use. Waterproof and very strong, it was capable of bonding a joint stronger than the parent wood, a tremendous step forward for the plywood industry: de-lamination had been one of its worst features prior to using this new adhesive.

Casein cement had been the approved adhesive in the aircraft industry during the 'thirties and at the start of the war. It had seemed eminently suited at the time, but was definitely inferior to this new synthetic adhesive. This was proven when early de Havilland Mosquito aircraft, in which casein cement was used, were sent to the Far East. They began having serious problems. The casein cement in humid atmosphere soon started to attract mould spores that caused it to deteriorate rapidly.

Termites and insects also enjoyed making a meal of the timber where it had become impregnated with the starch rich glue.

At the start of the war, Andrew Oliver had been drafted into the Royal Air Force and posted to the Royal Aircraft Establishment at Farnborough to help with research projects. It was only a short stay. One morning he was told to report to his Commanding Officer: he was to be demobbed immediately to return to High Wycombe to take up a new appointment. He was to report directly to Lord Beaverbrook, the Minister of Aircraft Production. This sudden development had been brought about when the firm of Venesta, a large specialist plywood manufacturer based in the East End of London, had been badly damaged during bombing raids early in the war. Quantity plywood production was almost at a standstill. It was decided that any equipment that could be salvaged would be re- located immediately to High Wycombe. Further specialist plywood presses were also to be relocated from Duxford and the Bristol Aeroplane Company. Equipment already available in Wycombe would be put at his disposal, and this included any from his foster father's company.

He found suitable premises for production at Kingsmead Road, Loudwater, on the site more recently occupied by Lintafoam. Some employees from Venesta were relocated to the town to help establish production.

Andrew assisted directly in some wooden aeroplane development, advising on the best utilisation of plywood in design and manufacture. This included spending many hours at Salisbury Hall on the early development of the prototype de Havilland 98 Mosquito. (The prototype can still be seen at its birthplace in the de Havilland Heritage Centre at Salisbury Hall.) He was able to assist in the pre-manufacture of plywood panels that could be made ready to fit, generating savings in time and cost and also minimising material wastage. Many aircraft ply panels, for reasons of strength, are made with the grain running diagonally, typically as seen on the rear fuselage of the Mosquito.

Some work building gliders, for which ply would form the major part of the structure, was undertaken at factories in Wycombe. One type was the Airspeed Hotspur, a small training glider, another the General Aircraft Horsa, a much larger glider, capable of carrying twenty-five fully equipped troops, or a light tank or field gun. Many curved ply sections, typically leading edges for the wings and tailplanes, were pre-formed for these and also for the Miles Magister and Master as well as the de Havilland Mosquito. As the war continued, Andrew became involved in crash inspection of any aircraft having timber construction. This also enabled him to keep track of German developments.

Towards the end of the war, a standard Dakota aircraft (KG 782) was converted into a flying office and conference room for Air Chief Marshal Sir Arthur "Bomber" Harris, G.C.B. He was Commander in Chief of R.A.F. Bomber Command, a position he had held since February 1942. Andrew Oliver led a team from Walter Baker, fitting it out with a luxury interior, using Indian laurel veneered ply panels with white mottled sycamore window surrounds and pelmets. The complete conversion, with a galley at the forward end, a central large saloon and a rear baggage compartment, was completed in four weeks and two days.

THE LAVISH INTERIOR OF THE DAKOTA AIRCRAFT

Photo TRADA

In a letter to Messrs Walter F. Baker, the Air Chief Marshal complimented them on their fine craftsmanship, making special reference to Mr. Andrew Oliver. This lavishly furnished interior had taken him full circle; back to doing the job he knew and loved. He continued in the quality ply and veneer trade for the rest of his life. Even in retirement, still respected as a fine craftsman, he continued to enjoy producing fine marquetry work.

THE LATE ANDREW OLIVER IN RETIREMENT.
Photo Mrs. Oliver

Understandably, an aura of secrecy, which continued long after the war, surrounded all the Mosquito work. Those who had worked so hard producing all the parts required had learnt never to talk about it. In many of the factories there were posters warning them not to talk about their work when outside the factory. Signs declaring CARELESS TALK COSTS LIVES were prominently displayed.

"An example of this secrecy and how well it worked was to become obvious when a friend showed me photos they had found amongst the belongings of a deceased relative. He had been one of the Styles brothers at Styles & Mealings factory in Ogilvie Road, High Wycombe. I was told they were "photos of the gliders made in Wycombe during the war". To emphasise the point while being shown a photo of a lorry ready to leave the factory with a fuselage on the back, I was told, 'Look it hasn't got an engine on the front so it must be a glider.'

To me even at this stage the beautiful streamline shape of the Mosquito fuselage was easily recognised. (See Styles and Mealing photographs.) Other photos taken inside the factory show fuselages being made in two halves. This was a very clever and convenient production method, facilitating the installation of many interior components before they were put together. Electrical cables, hydraulic pipes and flying controls, all so much easier to install than having to crawl down the confined interior of a fuselage."

(I.C.S.)

Hamilcar glider parts were made in Styles & Mealing. Was this deliberately used to mislead anyone trying to find out exactly what was going on? To the enemy, a rumour that they were employed in making gliders held none of the threat when compared with the destructive power of the new and top secret Mosquito.

Even after the war was over, the reluctance to talk about it remained. A man who had worked in the Dancer & Hearne factory throughout the war explained, "When it was all over and many of our old comrades returned, we did not like to talk about it. What had we really done compared with those who had been in the thick of it. What had we to be proud of in our protected jobs? So many who joined the fighting forces never returned."

Heathland Furniture in Copyground Lane, High Wycombe, the firm owned by J. (Jack) B. Heath, specialised in manufacturing the Mosquito wing rear spar, probably one of the more demanding tasks undertaken on this aircraft. The finished spar was over 50ft. in length and swept forward and upward from the centre. The booms, top and bottom members of the box section, were made with vertical laminations of Sitka Spruce 0.4" thick, travelling from wing tip to wing tip. A laminated ash reinforcing member was fixed to the centre of the inside face of the top boom. The top and bottom booms were placed into a jig, then the spacers fitted between them and the ply facings glued and screwed to the booms competing the box structure. (See J. B. Heath or J. Parker photos of the rear spar to appreciate the size and shape of this component.)

Throughout the war there was always pressure to increase production. A typical example of this and how it can go tragically wrong was at the Heathland works. A new method was suggested, to help reduce the time taken shaping each spar boom after laminating. Its gradually tapering shape was originally done by hand, planing the spar boom to size, a long and laborious process. In principle, using the new method, the surplus timber could be removed in one pass, using a specially adapted spindle machine. It required special large cutters and large guide bearings fitted to the spindle. Shaping templates were fitted to the laminated booms to guide it onto the bearings and past the cutters. The first time this was tried all was made ready and the templates fitted to both sides of the spar to guide it past the spindle. A team of men was assembled to feed it past the spindle (remember, it is fifty feet long). Their best spindle operator was responsible for ensuring it travelled past those lethal cutters accurately. Something or somebody slipped! The spindle operator lost his four fingers in those lethal cutters; they were all badly shaken. (Wood working machinery can always be dangerous and the spindle machine especially so.) No doubt at the time, some very choice words were used about the people who thought up that new method.

At first it looked as though this method would never be used. Certainly there were no volunteers to take that man's place. Next day it was Jack Heath himself who, taking off his jacket and rolling up his sleeves, took on the job. Before long, confidence returned, after which it was seen as yet one more of those unfortunate accidents that happened from time to time in the furniture industry. This operation did save many hours of hand shaping that was otherwise required. The first spar (using hand shaping) had taken 90 hours to produce. With the new method and other clever ideas, eventually it was reduced to 9 hours per spar. In an article in the Bucks Free Press on 29th September 1989, Jack Heath himself closes his article explaining about the work carried out during the wartime with a statement that they had produced parts for 5,570 Mosquito aircraft in this town – a remarkable contribution from what was then a small market town. In those days over 70% of the town's workforce was employed in the furniture factories.

Parker-Knoll, High Wycombe (then F Parker & Sons) were kept very busy with Mosquito part production. In 1943/44, they also became involved in repair work on Airspeed Horsa gliders. Glider pilot training was responsible for much of the damage done to these. None the less, many were repairable if suitable labour and facilities could be found, so they too arrived at Parker's. Not until mid-1944 were many to have their final flight, used during the D-Day invasion of Normandy. Many members of the Glider Pilot Regiment completed their initial training at R.A.F. Booker. (Now Wycombe Air Park.)

More components for the Mosquito were produced at the E. Gomme Spring Gardens factory. Included in the collection of de Havilland photographs held in the British Aerospace Archives at Farnborough is one showing tailplanes being sprayed. It is the only reference found showing these parts being produced in High Wycombe. The picture is quite unique in another way: in the background are the first items of post war furniture production (wardrobes). Yes, the change over in many of our factories was that quick!

Many women are seen working on aircraft parts in these photographs. This was often arduous and dirty work carried out in a fume-filled atmosphere, a situation common in many industries throughout the country. All single women, married women with no children and women over their child-caring years were compelled to help in war work, with the desperately needed production demands. It is almost impossible to imagine the situation today. Workers of the right skills, male or female, would

be dispatched to a new place of work at very short notice. They were left to find somewhere to live and report for work at a stipulated time: failing to report could lead to their arrest. Yet Mr. Oliver of Walter Baker, then in charge of all aircraft plywood production, considered some as nothing more than skivers, trying to avoid conscription, claiming the ability in any trade rather than be compelled to join the armed forces. Yet there can be no denying that, with quality control being under ministry inspectors, aircraft parts produced in this town were of the very highest standard, far above that expected of normal furniture workers. Certificates were issued to prove each part had passed strict ministry inspection standards at each production stage. This certificate had to accompany all parts until the aircraft was completed.

Just prior to the war, Castle Brothers had a new factory built on the developing Cressex Industrial Estate. One of the town's more progressive firms, it moved from the Wycombe valley in 1938/9. The management had great expectations of this thoroughly modern purpose-built factory. Yet this was all thwarted when they became involved in negotiations with the Airscrew Company of Weybridge, a manufacturer of wooden propellers. Conflicting opinions of what constituted a fair rent caused the Weybridge company to apply for a government backed compulsory order, requisitioning the factory.

These new premises were deemed ideal for the production of urgently needed wooden propellers. A struggle followed to obtain a fair rent, never settled to Jack Castle's satisfaction. He was then told he would be given the position of General Manager, having responsibility for the efficient running and maintenance of the factory (that he owned!). The other directors, who were offered nothing, voted that he be removed from the Castle's payroll while he was in the pay of this other firm. When returned at the end of the war, that new factory, equipped as it had been with all new machinery and modern equipment, was in a sad state, having been worked twenty-four hours a day, seven days a week for much of the war period. Subsequently the company never seemed to recover from this loss of income.

Castle's factory was re-named Airscrew Developments for this period of the war. It employed many of the town's craftsmen to produce aircraft propellers, always a very demanding task. The people employed were mostly those recognised for their skill within the trade. In the production of an individual propeller blade the highly stressed root section was made of a product known as "Jicwood", a material made up of highly compressed birch laminations. This was scarfed to spruce boards of natural density to form a complete blade, then roughly shaped on a copy lathe following a master pattern. Final shaping and balancing was achieved by hand crafting. Blades at this stage were checked for weight and matched up in sets that were fixed to the hub with hollow, steel root blade adapters.

In the early 1960s, Castle Bros. were taken over by E. Gomme Ltd. (makers of the well-known G-Plan range of furniture). It was a sad end to one of the town's largest furniture firms.

Before this, in the 1950s, William Birch, another of the town's large furniture factories, had been absorbed into the Gomme organisation. They were situated next to the E. Gomme factory, in Leigh Street. They too became involved making many of the Mosquito parts. At the County Museum Archives there is a report of a misdemeanour that nearly led to a charge of sabotage being bought against them, because a worker had inserted some paper into a joint to bring it up to the correct dimension, which was apparently found during inspection. At the end of the inquiry and after testing the joint it was found that because the resin glue had completely impregnated the paper, the joint remained as strong as it would have been had it been made correctly.

That was an interesting result, demonstrating how good the resin glue was, though gap filling was never considered one of its best attributes. From this record it appears that no further action was taken but it had certainly done nothing to improve their relationship with de Havilland. Subsequently there seemed to be continuing conflict on work undertaken by Birch for de Havilland, leading to claims that they were being underpaid for work done. Yet the counter claim from de Havilland implied they were taking too long completing the work, using inappropriate methods and jigs. Birch counter-claimed that they had been given insufficient information on these issues. Some of the comments after the First World War come to mind, when the furniture bosses claimed that they had made nothing out of their experience with the aviation business.

Photographs from the collection of Dancer & Hearne (probably the most complete set from any of the Wycombe firms involved) show the process of making the Mosquito main spar, the principal component made by them. Others depict the top wing skins being built up with Douglas Fir stringers sandwiched between two birch ply panels. The assembly of the fin is also well documented as it was being built, from the fin posts, ribs and leading edge being made and assembled, then finally covered with a ply skin. Of all the Wycombe firms, they had the longest

association with the de Havilland Enterprise and continued with aircraft work well into the fifties. Their expertise then expanded to include jig and presswork for many of the other British aircraft organisations. Vampire and Venom fuselages were the last major components manufactured for de Havilland. These also had the ply / balsa wood sandwich construction as used on the Mosquito.

Their principal factory was in Lindsay Avenue, with another in the village of Penn Street. Cecil Hearne was a great friend of Jack Heath, owner of the previously mentioned Heathland Furniture works. An article submitted to the Bucks Free Press by Jack Heath in 1989, explaining their wartime efforts, also gives a very interesting insight into their light-hearted attitude to some of the wartime regulations. At the end of the day they would often go together for a late drink at the Hit and Miss pub, where the Hearne family held the licence for some years. This was next to Cecil Hearne's other factory in Penn Street. They travelled by car with bits of Mosquito on the back seat, always ready to claim they were on business should they be stopped. It was illegal then to use vehicles for anything other than business purposes. Petrol could only be obtained with government-issued coupons, very strictly controlled.

The DH 103 Hornet, a single seat fighter in many ways similar to the Mosquito, was developed late in the war. A concrete fuselage mould was found on the railway embankment near Gomme's Spring Gardens factory. This mould is now at the de Havilland Heritage Centre at Salisbury Hall. These fuselages were possibly some of the last aircraft parts made at Gommes. The firm of Joynson and Holland, which still survives today, and Cam Tools also manufactured Mosquito parts.

Some furniture firms changed over to producing metal products. The Croxson Brothers' new factory in Queen Alexandra Road was requisitioned by the Ministry of Aircraft Production (MAP) in 1941, for the Heston Aircraft Co. Ltd. who were sub-contracted to Vickers Supermarine, manufacturers of the Wellington bomber and the Spitfire. Aluminium engine cowlings, bomb racks, bomb rack beams and bomb-bay doors (all for the Wellington), Mosquito engine nacelles, Spitfire flaps and ailerons were all produced there. A technical Manager and some skilled metal workers were sent from Heston to instruct the furniture workers in manufacturing these products. Another firm, F. Mealing in Ogilvie Road, produced tubular steel engine bearers and Mosquito exhaust stubs. Their employees had obviously been taught to weld to a high standard. Beatonson, who took over Andrews

Boatyard at Bourne End, manufactured Spitfire wing ribs.

High Duty Alloys and a Ministry of Aircraft Production site were both located in Coronation Road on the Cressex Estate. The former, whose parent company was in Slough, specialised in the manufacture and machining of lightweight magnesium alloy castings for aircraft wheel hubs, undercarriage struts and other components. The latter site had been the new furniture factory of A. J. Way. It was taken over by MAP to relocate the firm of Hydro Dividers from Westcliff-on-Sea, Essex, who were producing undercarriage legs for various bomber aircraft and miscellaneous Spitfire parts, including seats, trim tabs, fuel pumps and. many other cast and fabricated items.

Plastalune, located next to the Flint Cottage Public House, opposite the entrance to Wycombe railway station, produced many perspex components, such as cockpit canopies and gun turrets. Up to 150 staff were employed there. They also made the wooden moulds required for forming of these parts.

Davenport Vernon, the town's largest garage, whose imposing front entrance faced onto the High Street (now the Argos catalogue shop), undertook fuselage refurbishment of Vickers Wellington bombers. Their extensive covered premises were ideal for this purpose and included two large workshops stretching back behind the Library, Town Hall and Police Station to the bank of the river. This is now the area where the Swan Theatre stands. In 1940 the first of the workshops was converted to accommodate four Wellington fuselages, thus establishing a recognised repair depot.

The workforce was drawn from all occupations and walks of life – the works manager was an opera singer and they counted among their number ex-costermongers, fairground workers, school leavers and persons who had been relocated for war work.

Many of the fuselages arriving for repair had suffered a "wheels up" landing and had extensive damage to the underside.

The engines, wings and tail components were stripped off either at the crash site or the Maintenance Unit, only the fuselage arriving at Davenport Vernon on a sixty-foot long trailer known as a Queen Mary. At the start of the contract, the first of these attempted to enter the garage via the High Street but unfortunately it had insufficient room to manoeuvre and knocked down the traffic lights at the end of the High Street. It knocked them down again on the way out! Later deliveries were via the back entrance, alongside the Police Station.

On arrival they were stripped of their gun turrets, bomb doors, hydraulic, electric and oxygen systems and all fabric covering. This allowed a full assessment of any structural damage. The fuselage was placed into a jig to check its alignment. Damaged parts were replaced and new or refurbished components installed. It was then ready for fabric covering and initial doping, after which it was ready to be returned to be rebuilt into a fully serviceable aeroplane.

WORKERS AT THE DAVENPORT VERNON GARAGE assembled in front of this completely refurbished Vickers Wellington fuselage as it prepares to depart.

Photo Gerry V Tyack,
Wellington Aviation Museum, Moreton-in-Marsh.

In this period when Davenport Vernon were involved with the important work of repairing Wellington fuselages, they were often unable to continue with their vehicle repair work having neither labour nor space. A statement placed in the BFP on 16th February 1945 showed their great desire to get back to normal. Unfortunately reproducing pictures from the B.F.P. is never very good but the row of fuselages under repair shows how they were otherwise engaged.

Their press release stated, "The war has claimed so much of the personal attention we gave to our customers in happier times. Some hundreds of these fuselages and components have passed through our hands for repair, to play their part again in Britain's gigantic air operations. A separate department also has turned out quantities of sub-assemblies. In our Vehicle Repair Shops every endeavour has been made to offer an efficient service. We gratefully acknowledge our customers' co-operation and their understanding of present conditions. This has been a great incentive to our staff, whose skill and efforts, despite shortages of materials and manpower, have kept large numbers of essential vehicles in service.

We confidently look forward to the time when the experience gained by all in this firm, assisted by the return of valued employees from the services, will enable us to offer a more fully comprehensive sales and service organisation than ever before."

This is the reason —

DAVENPORT VERNON & Co. LTD.
31, 32 & 34 HIGH STREET,   HIGH WYCOMBE.   Phone 446/7

DAVENPORT VERNON AFTER THE WAR returned to the sales and service of motor vehicles, still having their prominent site on Wycombe High Street, today the site of the Argos

AN AERIAL PHOTOGRAPH OF HIGH WYCOMBE TOWN CENTRE, taken with a Vinten "Eagle" camera in 1944, one of a series of photographs taken from a Mosquito P/R aircraft.

THE VINTEN "EAGLE" AERIAL CAMERA

The Vinten "Eagle" Aerial cameras were assembled at the Norman Reeves showroom and garage at Crendon House. They were the local Ford car dealers situated just below the High Wycombe railway station on the corner of Birdcage Walk.

This camera was considered the finest of its type and responsible for many of those very fine photographs taken by photo-reconnaissance squadrons based at R.A.F. Benson. Film development and processing was carried out at R.A.F. Medmenham.

IN MEMORY

Travelling through the town today, little remains to remind us of those war years. In comparison with some other towns, Wycombe was fortunate having suffered no large scale air attacks. Yet one part still holds within the names of its roads at least a tribute to some of those wartime aircraft.

Roads on Cressex Industrial Estate, completed just after the war, were named after bomber aircraft of the time, the three heavy four-engined bombers, Lancaster, Stirling and Halifax, two earlier twin-engined bombers, the Wellington and Blenheim, and lastly three aircraft, all developed from the Lancaster, the Lincoln, York and Shackleton.

CHAPTER 5

AIRCRAFT PRODUCTION PHOTOGRAPHS

A series of photos that show the extent of work undertaken in the furniture factories of High
Wycombe during the Second World War.

DANCER & HEARNE BROS. LTD.
LINDSAY AVENUE, HIGH WYCOMBE.

DANCER & HEARNE STAFF GROUP
One of the first factories in the town to start producing Mosquito parts.
Photo BAE SYSTEMS.

MANY WING MAIN SPARS WERE PRODUCED HERE

FINISHED MAIN SPARS stacked at the end of the production department are fifty feet long and maintained within
an accuracy of 0.040 of an inch. (1mm). The following pages illustrate their production.
Photo BAE SYSTEMS.

BULK TIMBER ARRIVING AT THE FACTORY being carefully checked in. This is specially selected Sitka spruce, straight and close grained, both strong and light, from the west-coast region of North America. At the time, the merchant ships carrying cargoes across the Atlantic ocean were in continuous peril from German submarines (U Boats), which hunted in packs and sank many thousand of tons of allied shipping.

Photo BAE SYSTEMS.

CONVERTING THE BULK TIMBER Here it is being sawn to thickness for the laminations that make up the spar booms, initially cut oversize, then planed to 0.4in. (10mm) thick. Two booms are required in each spar, one at the top and one at the bottom. These are joined with two birch ply web faces to form a box section.

Photo BAE SYSTEMS.

Box section of a spar.

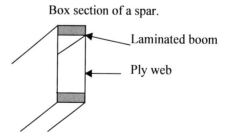

Laminated boom

Ply web

THE PLANED LAMINATIONS ARE INSPECTED AND SCARFS CUT, allowing them to be joined to form the lengths required (scarf joint: the tapering of the end or edge of timber to form an overlapping joint; the taper angle on the these spar laminations is 1:15).

Photo BAE SYSTEMS.

GLUE PREPARATION WAS CAREFULLY CONTROLLED, being weighed and mixed, then distributed in coloured containers. The coloured time indicators on the wall show the time that the glue in the matching pots must no longer be used. Mrs. Oxlade and Mr. Buss ensured that a constant supply was always at hand. At first the glue used was casein cement, a milk derivative. In tropical climates this starch-rich product became a breeding medium for mould spores and attracted termites and other wood-devouring insects. It was later replaced with a newly-developed urea formaldehyde resin glue.

Photo BAE SYSTEMS.

BOOM LAMINATIONS ARE LAID UP READY FOR GLUING, a very messy job. The men needed no hooks to hang up their aprons at the end of the day, as they would be stiff enough to stand up on their own

Photo BAE SYSTEMS.

Placing the glued laminations in the jig and tightening down the screw cramps to ensure contact along the full length of the glue joints.

Photo BAE SYSTEMS.

ONE EDGE TRIMMED SQUARE ON THE BANDSAW. This operation then allows it to be planed to the required width.

Photo BAE SYSTEMS.

THE TWO LAMINATED SPAR BOOMS have been placed in the jig and the spacers are being fitted and glued in place. On the far side of the bench the birch ply webs have been fitted and the rib posts (where the wing ribs fit during the wing assembly operation) are being screwed on.

Photo BAE SYSTEMS.

VIEW OF A SPAR CONSTRUCTION BEFORE APPLYING THE PLY WEB. Note the thickened centre of the bottom boom; this is the part seen being trimmed on the bandsaw. Three more laminations are added to this, extending it to the wingtips.

Photo BAE SYSTEMS.

SPAR FRONT FACE. Reinforcing members are being fitted, including reinforcing blocks in areas where the undercarriage and engines are to be fitted.

Photo BAE SYSTEMS.

THE BORING JIG, where the holes are bored for the attachment bolts to secure the engines and undercarriage. This is the final operation before they are stacked at the end of the workshop ready for dispatch (see second photo). Initially the production rate was about seven per week. As the workers became more experienced, better production methods evolved and it soon rose to fourteen, eventually peaking at nineteen/ twenty per week.

Photo BAE SYSTEMS.

FINISHED SPARS ARE LOADED FOR THEIR JOURNEY to the next production stage, where it will be assembled into the wing structure. Supervising at the rear is Mr. Pierce, the Works Manager. At the side of the lorry (known as a Queen Mary) is a Special Constable who always travelled with the lorry.

Photo BAE SYSTEMS.

DANCER & HEARNE

PRODUCTION OF THE WING SKINS

THESE WERE COMPOSITE ITEMS CONSISTING OF BIRCH PLY AND DOUGLAS FIR STRINGERS.

TOP SKIN. BIRCH PLY PANELS, scarfed together to form a one-piece skin, the outer panels being diagonal-grained. On the bench the bridge cramps press down on the scarf joints while the glue sets.

Photo BAE SYSTEMS.

DOUGLAS FIR STRINGERS and other spacers laid out on the wing skin jig and carefully held in place until fitted with the ply top skin.

Photo BAE SYSTEMS

WORKERS SCREW THE PLY PANEL ONTO THE STRINGERS, speed being essential to secure the panel before the glue sets. The glue is applied to the whole inner face of the panel, which in addition to being an adhesive also serves as a waterproof coating for the interior of the birch plywood.

Photo BAE SYSTEMS.

PRODUCING THE FIN

THE FIN SHOP. Along the left-hand wall are the jigs for assembling the fin structure. On the right, women are making the fin ribs. Around the shop several racks can be seen holding the completely assembled fins.

Photo BAE SYSTEMS.

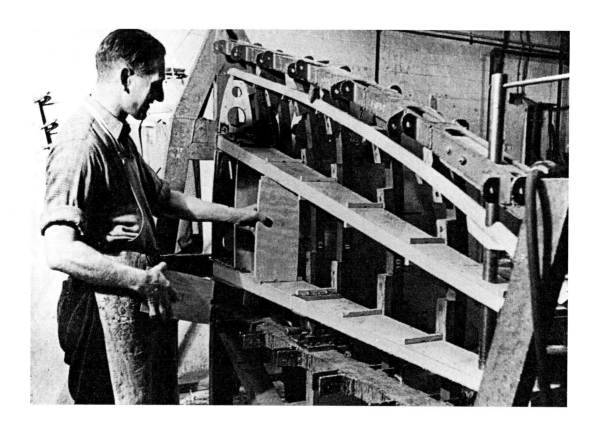

THE FIN STRUCTURE is being assembled in its jig. The leading edge and two spars are held while the ribs are glued and inserted into position.

Photo BAE SYSTEMS.

DOPING ON THE MADAPALAM FABRIC (finest Egyptian cotton) The lady to the right is carefully checking for imperfections before applying the covering to the fin. The fins stood to the left are still to be covered. Two against the wall and the one on trestles, left front, have been covered. The fabric is applied with red dope, a cellulose based paint.

Photo BAE SYSTEMS.

WILLIAM BIRCH LTD

LEIGH STREET, HIGH WYCOMBE

A MEETING AT WILLIAM BIRCH LTD between their management and personnel from de Havilland in June 1945. In March of that year they had been told there would be no more orders. The last one appears to have been for bomb doors on 17th May 1944, which was either cancelled or completed in September 1945.   Photo BAE SYSTEMS

PICTURE OF WILLIAM BIRCH LTD taken, according to the records, on 13th August 1943. It shows the upper wing skins being constructed. On the left, ply skin panels are drilled for screws that fix it to the stringers laid out on the right.
Photo BAE SYSTEMS.

DANCER & HEARNE

PRODUCTION OF THE AIRSPEED OXFORD COCKPIT FLOOR

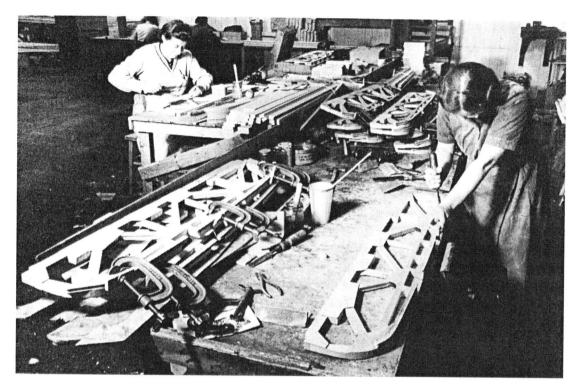

MASS PRODUCING THE COCKPIT UNDER-FLOOR FORMERS.

Photo BAE SYSTEMS.

INSPECTION STAGE. All parts are inspected before being assembled into the floor structure.

Photo BAE SYSTEMS.

FLOOR ASSEMBLY JIG. This angled jig emulates the position of the floor in the aircraft, thus ensuring the under-floor formers are held vertically.

Photo BAE SYSTEMS.

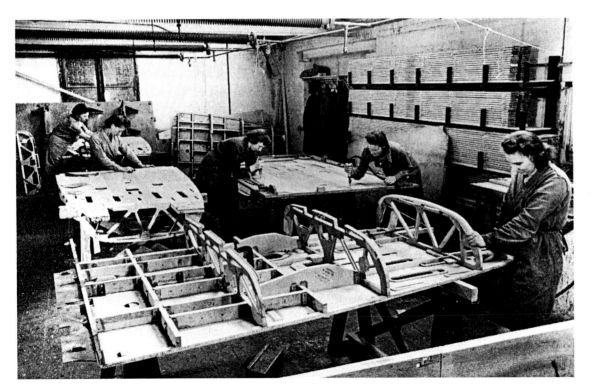

FINAL DETAIL FINISHING TO COMPLETE THE FLOOR.

Photo BAE SYSTEMS.

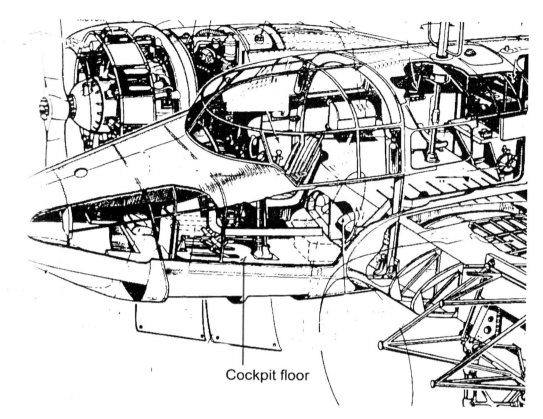

A CUTAWAY VIEW OF AN AIRSPEED OXFORD, SHOWING THE COCKPIT FLOOR

DANCER & HEARNE

VAMPIRE FUSELAGE PRODUCTION

THE NEW JET-PROPELLED DE HAVILLAND VAMPIRE. At the end of World War Two, the production of fuselage halves for the Vampire was under way. These were the same ply/balsa/ply sandwich construction as the Mosquito.

Photo – TRADA.

LEFT: An excellent example of the DH Vampire fuselage. The two halves are together and many of the other wooden components like the laminated cockpit coaming and air intake frame are fitted. In the side the square hole will be the battery compartment and at the front, a lid, which will form the upper half of the nose and allow access to radio/radar equipment

BELOW: laminations being cramped together to form the air intake coaming.

FUSELAGE HALF READY TO BE REMOVED FROM THE MOULD

Photos - TRADA

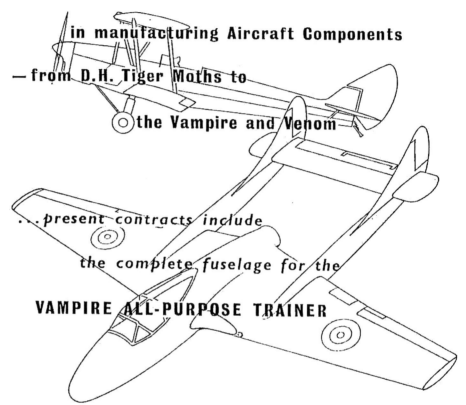

We have many years' experience

in manufacturing Aircraft Components

— from D.H. Tiger Moths to

the Vampire and Venom

...present contracts include

the complete fuselage for the

VAMPIRE ALL-PURPOSE TRAINER

We also specialise in ASSEMBLY JIGS & FIXTURES · BLANK & PIERCE TOOLS · MILLING FIXTURES

HUFFORD & RUBBER PRESS DIES and are assisting in tooling the following aircraft

GLOSTER JAVELIN	FAIREY GANNET	D.H. COMET	VICKERS VALIANT	HAWKER HUNTER	AVRO VULCAN

DANCER & HEARNE BROS LTD.

Lindsay Avenue, High Wycombe, Bucks. Tel : High Wycombe 1242

AN ADVERT IN *"THE AEROPLANE"* OF THE 4TH SEPTEMBER 1953, giving the details of Dancer & Hearne's continuing involvement in the aircraft industry. "NERO" was their well-known trade mark.

STYLES & MEALING LTD

OGILVIE ROAD, HIGH WYCOMBE

Another of the Wycombe family firms, their production ability was second to none. They were still fulfilling Government contracts for office-type furniture and fittings until 1965. They were taken over by G.E.C. to make radio cabinets. The following pictures show their involvement making Mosquito parts.

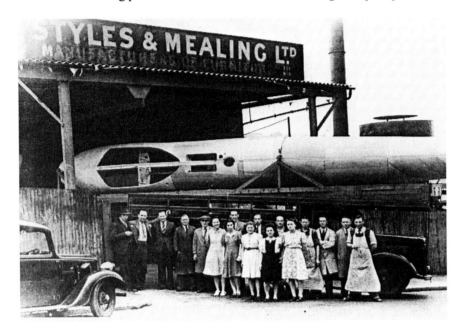

MEMBERS OF THE STAFF FROM STYLES & MEALING LTD. stand in front of a Mosquito fuselage mounted on a specially adapted lorry ready to be taken to the next stage of its construction.

Photo. Bob Mead.

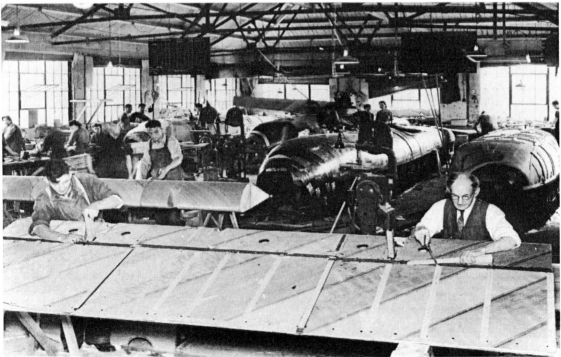

FUSELAGE HALVES BEING PRODUCED ON THEIR JIGS. In front are completed flaps. Note the diagonal-grain ply often used on this type of structure.

Photo. Bob Mead.

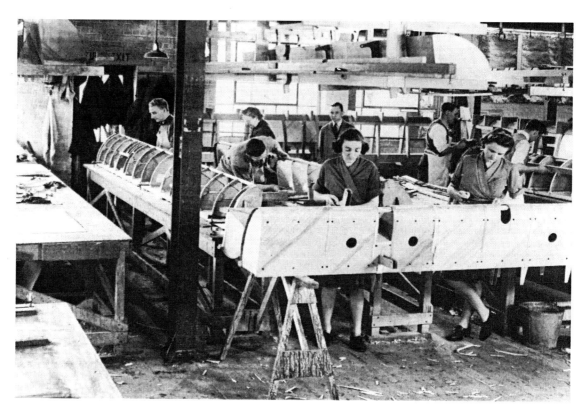

FLAP LEADING EDGES. On the bench the ribs are assembled into the
structure which is ply-covered as seen in the foreground.

Photo. Bob Mead.

FLAP ASSEMBLY JIGS. The flap leading edge is placed at the bottom and the ribs are then attached,
forming the inner and outer flap, at this stage still all in one piece.

Photo. Bob Mead.

TWO FUSELAGE HALVES having interior work carried out. At this stage, threaded ferrules for mounting system components are glued and inserted into the fuselage skin.

Photo. Bob Mead.

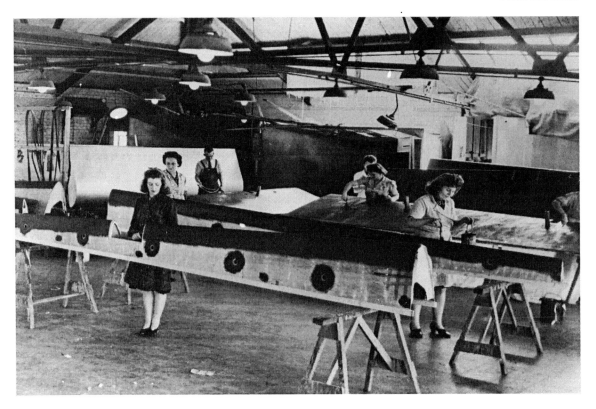

WING LEADING EDGES. Being covered with fabric held on with red cellulose dope always applied by hand. Several coats were required before being sprayed with a silver coat, used to protect against ultra violet sun rays which could cause the fabric to decay. It was then ready for its camouflage finish.

Photo. Bob Mead.

STYLES & MEALING LTD

JUNE 1973
THE SAD END
TO ANOTHER OF WYCOMBE'S
FURNITURE FACTORIES

Not long after the take-over by G.E.C. a fire swept the entire building. It was completely gutted and never rebuilt.

Furniture firms were by their very nature a fire hazard, having a great deal of timber in different stages of manufacture on the premises. Sawdust, shavings and highly inflammable polishes could soon change a workplace into a blazing inferno.

Unfortunately this was a scene repeated many times in the town's history.

Photos - BFP/ Andrew Mealing

J. B. HEATH (Heathland Furniture)

COPYGROUND LANE, HIGH WYCOMBE

Photo - ERIC HEATH.

J. B. (JACK) HEATH was the owner of the Wycombe family business that helped to build the prosperity of the town and its reputation for fine furniture. During the Second World War they were soon involved with helping to build the de Havilland Mosquito, making over five thousand rear spars.

This picture from an album entitled *'Heathland Endeavour 1942-45'* explains: 'Many of the (Wycombe) factories worked in aircraft production, making wooden propellers, the main parts of the Tiger Moth and above all, components for the famous de Havilland Mosquito, most of which was manufactured at Wycombe.' This photograph shows the edge boom department at the Heathland factory.

How well this portrays the sheer size of this single part, the wing rear spar, approximately 50 feet long. It is one of the most difficult components to make, having both forward and upward sweep built into its length.

The machine in the foreground looking like an old-fashioned mangle is a hand-driven glue spreader. The rollers rest in a trough of glue, depositing it on the timber as it passes through. In the background are the cramping jigs where the spar booms are built up with these laminations of spruce timber.

Photo - ERIC HEATH..

In these jigs the top and bottom spar booms are brought together with spacers between and the ply webs fitted to complete the box structure of the spar.

Photo - ERIC HEATH.

THE DINGHY BOXES that fit into the top of the fuselage just behind the cockpit canopy of the Mosquito. This oblong opening can be seen in the first Styles and Mealings picture.

F. PARKER & SONS Ltd

TEMPLE END, HIGH WYCOMBE (later to become **Parker Knoll**)

THE LEADING EDGE STRUCTURE OF THE MOSQUITO WING. On the trestles in the foreground are sets of leading edge ribs, being made by the ladies. On the right of the picture are the pre-formed ply skins.

Photo BAE SYSTEMS.

A REAR SPAR NOW REMOVED FROM THE JIG AND BEING FINISHED OUT BY HAND

Photo   BAE SYSTEMS

THE WING TANKS USED BY THE MOSQUITO, right foreground. These were of moulded wood laminations and internally coated with a fuel-proof lining. Behind, fuselage halves are being made.

Photo   BAE SYSTEMS

E. GOMME LTD

SPRING GARDENS WORKS, HIGH WYCOMBE.

MOSQUITO FUSELAGE HALVES, the main product from this large factory.

Photo   BAE SYSTEMS

This unique picture shows the last tailplanes passing through the spray shop and immediately following are the first furniture items (wardrobes) to be produced after the war. Most firms were glad to be back to their normal production. In the fifties this firm would be producing the newest fashion in furniture, the G-Plan range.

Photo. BAE SYSTEMS

E. GOMME Ltd.   AIRCRAFT.

REQUEST FOR OFFICIAL CLEARANCE.

To INSPECTOR IN CHARGE A.I.D.

SUBJECT....TOP....WING....PORT. R.T.O. REPORT No .... DATE....25th..July,..1940.

TIGER MOTH Mark 2.   Sub-Contract No. AP 7672.

The following Parts are now awaiting Inspection :—

ITEM REF. No.	PART No.	No. OFF	DESCRIPTION
2543.	U.3212. Mk. 2. Issue 6.	2	FINAL INSPECTION.
2546.	do.		do.

Remarks by A.I.D.

E. GOMME Ltd.   AIRCRAFT.

REQUEST FOR OFFICIAL CLEARANCE.

To INSPECTOR IN CHARGE A.I.D.

SUBJECT TOP WING STBD. R.T.O. REPORT No............ DATE August 8th. 1940.

TIGER MOTH Mark 2.   Sub-Contract No. AP 7672.

The following Parts are now awaiting Inspection :—

ITEM REF. No.	PART No.	No. OFF	DESCRIPTION
2954.	U.3213. Mk. 2. Issue 6.	2	FINAL INSPECTION.
2958.	do.		do.

Remarks by A.I.D.

Date cleared   - 9 AUG 1940   by   [A. I. D. J. 41]   A.I.D.

A.I.D. Certificates issued at E. Gomme Ltd for de Havilland Tiger Moth wings manufactured there during 1940.

A GROUP OF GOMME STAFF SIT IN FRONT OF A FINISHED MOSQUITO TAILPLANE.

Photo BAE SYSTEMS

WALTER BAKER LTD.

BELLFIELD APPROACH, HIGH WYCOMBE

WALTER BAKER, Wycombe's plywood and veneer specialists, were kept very busy. Here can be seen the cutting of birch laminates for producing diagonal-grained ply panels, so often preferred for the skinning of aircraft parts. To save waste, panels were made to the size required right from this initial stage. Photo BAE SYSTEMS.

CHAPTER 6

THE ALLIED BOMBER COMMANDS

AND THE SECRETS OF HUGHENDEN MANOR

Parts of this chapter, covering the RAF Bomber Command Headquarters and the USAAF Eighth Air Force Head Quarters, are drawn from the publication "*After the Battle*" No 87. Permission to reproduce these was kindly given by the Editor, Winston G. Ramsey.

ROYAL AIR FORCE BOMBER COMMAND HEADQUARTERS, HIGH WYCOMBE

Royal Air Force Bomber Command was formed on 14th July 1936, its first Air Officer Commanding-in-Chief (A.O.C.-in-C.) being Sir John Steel, with the initial headquarters at Uxbridge, west of London. Just over one year later, in September 1937, command passed to Sir Edgar Ludlow-Hewitt who returned from India to take up the appointment whilst a permanent site was sought for a headquarters for this new Command.

As one of the main R.A.F. training depots, Uxbridge was required for the induction of new recruits, leaving little space on the station for other activities, so Bomber Command found temporary accommodation at Bridge House in Richings Park, Langley, Buckinghamshire. Additional space was found at the nearby Actors' Orphanage, which was also requisitioned. Meanwhile, the search continued for a suitable site for a permanent headquarters.

"SOUTHDOWN"
(AS IT WAS INITIALLY CODE NAMED)

The siting of the Bomber Command HQ at High Wycombe is thought to have stemmed from a chance remark by Wing Commander Alan Oakeshott who was working at the Air Ministry when the search for a location was being undertaken. The Wing Commander had grown up in the village of Naphill in the Chiltern Hills where his father was a prominent local landowner. He suggested that as the HQ had to be in southern England and well screened by trees, the wooded slopes of the Chilterns around Walters Ash would be ideal. Not only was the area remote, but it lacked significant features when observed from the

air, which would make it difficult for an enemy to spot. He backed up his suggestions with photographs and a decision was soon made by the Directorate of Works to build at Walters Ash.

Before the Second World War, High Wycombe, 30 miles north-west of London, was known mainly for its chair-making industry, which was established in the area because of the extensive beech woods in the region. The town's seclusion in the rolling Chiltern Hills also made it an attractive proposition when RAF Bomber Command had completed its search for a suitable location for its headquarters. The site was as suggested north of the town at Walter's Ash (more commonly spelt now as Walters Ash) where the road from Naphill runs beside Park Wood. This tree cover was maintained as far as possible during the building works. This commenced in November 1938, the main contractors being John Laing and Son Ltd., although acquisition of all the land required was not finalised until 1940. Land for the main sites (Nos. 1 and 2 – some 90 acres), was compulsorily purchased from Bradenham Manor in May 1940. The area of site No. 3 was bought on 18th June 1940 from the Education Trust Foundation, and that for site No. 4 from the executors of the late Mr. C. W. Raffety of Walters Ash Farm on 12th September 1941.

An additional 11½ acres, added for officers' married quarters on 25th January 1940, purchased from Mrs. Ishbel Ridgley of Speen Farm, was eventually used for the erection of wireless transmitting aerials.

Laing's were instructed to complete the work, including the underground operations block, as soon as possible and a labour force some 500 strong moved in during 1938. Local rumour had it that it was a secret wartime site for the Houses of Parliament. One particular aspect of the work was the preservation of tree cover. Each tree was numbered so that every possible advantage could be gained from using natural camouflage. Any trees affected by the building work were supported and several new coppices planted. Grim's Ditch, an earthwork dating from around the 5th Century, which lay in the compound, was also preserved.

Site No. 1 was used for the command, administrative and office buildings, interconnected by underground tunnels, which were also to act as service ducts. Nearly 29,000 cubic feet of spoil was excavated to construct the underground operations block, sited 50 ft. below ground. It required the provision of 8,800 yards of waterproof concrete and 200 tons of reinforcement. The overhead protection was 20 ft. thick, consisting of a 5ft. 6in. roof slab covered with a layer of ballast, then a second 2ft. layer of concrete topped with a 4ft. layer of earth. On top of this was a 5ft. reinforced concrete burster slab extending beyond the walls of the bunker to detonate a direct hit. The whole structure was covered with earth and grassed over. Army guards patrolled the site from January 1940.

Site No. 2 was located in a partial clearing between Yewtree Hill Plantation and Falconer's Hill Wood. A wide avenue, known as the Queen's Ride, crossed the area, which had been established to commemorate the visit of Queen Elizabeth I.

Here the officers' married quarters were built together with a traditional pre-war style officers' mess, although this was built to look like a manor house standing in its own garden. The airmen's quarters were grouped on site No. 3 and included the sick quarters and NAAFI.

A house called Springfields at Great Kingshill, some five miles east of High Wycombe, was requisitioned in February 1940 for the personal residence of the A.O.C.-in-C, a direct line being installed from there to the operations room.

The G.P.O. began the installation of the communications equipment in October 1939, although extensive delays during the winter postponed a planned occupation date from the first week in February to 12th March 1940. The move from Richings Park was completed by the afternoon of the 15th. The new code name for the headquarters at Walters Ash was "SOUTHDOWN"; the first camp commandant was Wing Commander H. Dawes.

On 3rd April, Air Chief Marshal Sir Charles Portal took over from Air Chief Marshal Ludlow-Hewitt. Flying over the site to inspect it, the new commander promptly ordered that all flat concrete roofs must be camouflaged. He was also concerned about the well-worn footpaths leading to the anti-aircraft emplacements sited nearby which could give the game away to an astute enemy photo-interpreter.

On the outbreak of war, on paper, Bomber Command consisted of fifty-five squadrons split into six Groups, although there were no reserves and no training organisation. When ten squadrons were dispatched to France, they became known as the Advanced Air Striking Force, comprising two Wings of light bombers, mainly Blenheims and Battles. However at that stage British-based bombers were only permitted to drop propaganda leaflets or carry out restricted attacks on naval targets.

In August 1940, Air Chief Marshal Sir Richard Peirse took over as A.O.C.-in-C until illness forced his replacement by Air Marshal Sir Arthur Harris on 22nd February 1942. He was a practical airman, commanding No. 5 Group at the beginning of the war. Now he was to mastermind the implementation of a new phase in air operations against Germany, the new A.O.C.-in-C. being instructed to focus his operations on the morale of the enemy civil population and in particular, the main industrial areas.

This policy was adopted because the night attacks made by the RAF up to 1941 had proved disappointing. A Ministry report concluded that two thirds of the bombs dropped landed more than five miles from the target. To improve the situation it was decided to try using large formations of bombers sent to saturate an area, in the hope the target would be destroyed. This would only be possible if and when there were sufficient aircraft.

At the time this type of bombing was wasteful and expensive and still not guaranteed to destroy the intended target. It was referred to as "Carpet Bombing". Harris himself had no part in the formulation of this new directive (from mid-1941 he had been in charge of the RAF delegation in Washington), yet today misinformed public opinion still label him as the instigator. Nevertheless he pursued the policy with ruthless efficiency, an efficiency that earned him the title "Bomber Harris."

At "Southdown" in February 1942 a new building for the Operations Research Section was opened, with Harris in control. Within three months, the Command had mounted the first massive 1,000-bomber raid. Then in August, the Pathfinder Force was formed. This was a select group of pilot/navigator crews who were responsible for marking the targets before the arrival of the main bomber force. The effect was to greatly improve the accuracy of bomb concentration on any selected target. Both Lancaster and Mosquito aircraft were used in this role, but the Mosquito's ability to fly into the target area very low and extremely fast soon showed its superiority in this role. They were also legendary as bombers in their own right. There are many reports of their pinpoint bombing accuracy throughout the war.

THE LACEY GREEN AIRSTRIP

The essence of this article is drawn from *"The Lacey Green Story"* by Mike Osborn, of the Airfield Research Group, and published in their *Airfield Review* Magazine; also an article by Douglas Tilbury in *"Hallmark"* the Lacey Green and Loosley Row Magazine." Help and information have been received from Mr. J. West (the son of Dick West who ran the farm in 1944) and Mrs. West, who still reside at Stocken Farm.

We thank these for their help and their permission allowing us to use their material.

As D-Day (6th June 1944) approached, the H.Q. for the Combined or Allied Expeditionary Air Force was set up at Stanmore Park, Middlesex. It was equipped with a landing strip for light communications aircraft. As meetings with Bomber Command senior staff would be frequent during the coming months, rapid transportation between this site and the Bomber Command H.Q. was required. The journey by road between the two sites was a tedious cross country drive but by air it was just a quick 22-mile flight, therefore an airstrip as close as possible to Bomber Command H.Q. would be the answer. Until this time the Bomber Command H.Q. Communications Flight had been at Halton with three Auster Aircraft.

was invited to partake of a drink while discussing the matter with the A.O.C-in-C. Later he left quite happy with the explanation given, having been convinced that the incident had never happened. No doubt those who understood the A.O.C.-in-C. and his determination to get things done may have had a different opinion of this episode.

On the 1st June a suitable site was located at Stocken Farm, Lacey Green, just three quarters of a mile from Bomber Command H.Q., land farmed by the West family. They still farm this land today. Mrs. West is the author of a local book entitled *"A Chiltern Village School, Against all Odds, 1850-1930"*, based on the Lacey Green school diary. In it there are references to aircraft landing or crashing at Lacey Green during the First World War, though unfortunately none are identified.

On Saturday 3rd June, Mr. Richard West had his tea interrupted by a knock on his farmhouse door. There were three gentlemen, a Mr. R. Kimber, Wycombe District Divisional Officer of the Bucks War Agricultural Committee, Mr. G. H. Cox, from Waldridge Farm, and an Air Ministry official who introduced himself by saying, "We want the centre of your farm for a flying field." Within the hour a bulldozer would be arriving to start the work. They had been unable to pre-warn Mr. West because of the risk to security.

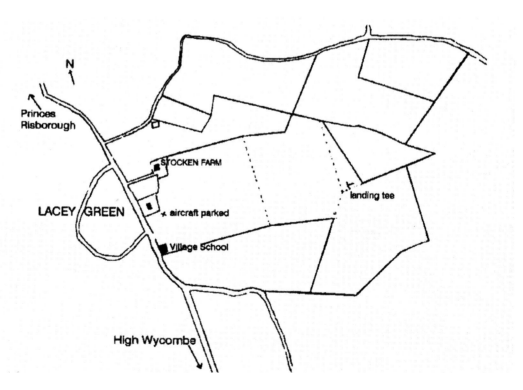

Prior to the building of the new airstrip, there had been tales in the village of an aircraft being landed occasionally on the main road that ran adjacent to the headquarters. A police officer who called at the headquarters to enquire into the matter

The initial project took forty-five acres of land, which was quickly cleared of trees and hedgerows including the felling of two clumps of horse chestnut trees and one clump of lime trees.

Three days later (D-Day), the first aircraft to take off from the new airstrip was a Stinson L5 Sentinel, piloted by Harris himself. This was his personal aircraft that was on a long-term loan from the United States Army Air Force (USAAF). This loan had apparently been arranged by General Doolittle, Commander in Chief of the United States Eighth Army Air Force, which had their headquarters at the nearby Wycombe Abbey. For the first weeks, flights from this airfield were fairly routine and local, mainly to Stanmore Park, but as the allied invasion forces moved further into Europe, flights to France became common events. The following year the airfield was extended to include another sixty-six acres of land. During this time the hard-pressed farmer was forced to sell off some of his stock: fifty breeding ewes and their lambs had to go. A generous offer from Mr. Cox, a neighbouring farmer, of twenty-five acres of land helped to keep him going.

The strip remained on charge to Bomber Command until February 1946. During that time, aircraft operating from there included: two Taylorcraft Austers; a D.H. Tiger Moth II (N9211); a D.H. Hornet Moth (W5748, ex civil G-ADKJ); a Miles Messenger I (RH369); a Percival Proctor III (HM480) and a Stinson L5 Sentinel (299015). The Messenger was the second of this type from the production line of the Miles factory at Woodley, near Reading and was delivered direct to Lacey Green. About the same time a similar aircraft became the personal aircraft for 'Monty', General Sir Bernard Montgomery, who had been appointed as Ground Commander of the Allied Armies (21st Army Group).

The Royal Air Force erected a blister hangar on the site. After their departure it was put to good use for various farming purposes during the late 'forties and early 'fifties. It was eventually dismantled in the 'seventies and taken away to be re-erected elsewhere.

Mr. Andrew Oliver, mentioned earlier, was by this time on Harris's personal staff as a "British Civilian Expert", with responsibility for examining all aircraft crashes involving wooden structures, checking all reports of failures through timber faults or glue failure. Wing Commander D. B. Smith, Harris's personal assistant, would often fly him to an airfield or crash site.

During the war period, three royal visits to the station are recorded. The Duke and Duchess of Gloucester made the first on the 26th October 1943. The Duchess, in her full uniform, held the rank of Air Chief Commandant of the Woman's Auxiliary Air Force (WAAF). Air Chief Marshal Sir Arthur Harris and the Senior (WAAF) Staff Officer, Group Officer L. M. Crowther, showed her around the site. His Majesty King George VI and Queen

Elizabeth visited on the 7th February 1944, when the function of the Operations Room was explained to them. A year later the Duchess of Kent made the last royal visit to the station during the war.

AIR CHIEF MARSHAL SIR ARTHUR HARRIS ESCORTS THE DUCHESS OF GLOUCESTER, CENTRE, AIR CHIEF COMMANDANT, WAAF, ON A TOUR OF THE HEADQUARTERS SITE, WITH SENIOR WAAF STAFF OFFICER, GROUP OFFICER L. M. CROWTHER, 26th OCTOBER 1943.

The hub of Bomber Command H.Q. was naturally the Operations Room, and the story is told that the staff below ground were always forewarned of the impending arrival of the A.O.C.-in-C. by the pre-arranged signal of sending a table-tennis ball down the Lamson pneumatic message tube.

Air Chief Marshal Harris remained at his post until September 1945, when he was replaced by Air Marshal Sir Norman Bottomley. His impending retirement from the service at the age of fifty-three was to be on the 15th November. Unfortunately this was announced in the newspapers in mid-August, some implying he had been sacked, which was certainly not the case.

Before retiring, a doctor friend, Air Vice Marshal T. J. Kelly, advised him to go to the RAF Hospital at Halton for a medical examination, which confirmed he was still suffering from a duodenal ulcer that had first been identified while serving in Palestine prior to the outbreak of war in 1939. He remained at the hospital for the whole of November for treatment. On the 9th January 1946 a medical board reported him considerably improved, sufficient to take an appointment in the temperate climate of Africa, where he hoped to take up residence in the near future, though his health problem had caused retirement to be deferred until the 4th February.

On the 1st January 1946, he had received his final reward from the RAF for his dedicated efforts as Commander of Bomber Command throughout those three and a half arduous war years, being promoted to the highest rank his service could bestow, Marshal of the Royal Air Force. Following this, on the 4th February at High Wycombe Town Hall he was made an Honorary Freeman of the town. In December 1951 he received a KGB (Knight Grand Cross of the Order of the Bath) and in the New Year's Honours List of 1953 he was created a Baron, with his chosen territorial designation of Chepping Wycombe. (Originally he had requested "High Wycombe".)

There had been much controversy at the time of his retirement (and there still is to this day) concerning his role in the mass bombing raids that had caused so much damage and destruction in Germany. Many were quite happy to let him shoulder the whole responsibility. An article in the Sunday Times of November 1960, based on a forthcoming publication of the memoirs of Earl Attlee, stated: "When reviewing the wartime military commanders, he considered Harris was not 'frightfully good', his bombing policy, especially that of attacking the German cities was not really worth while."

Understandably this prompted a sharp reply from Harris who usually ignored such statements. Writing to Attlee, he forcefully reminded him the truth of the matter was otherwise. "I am more than weary of repeated attempts by commission or omission, that have been made since the war to saddle me, and me alone, with the bombing policies ordered and approved by HM Government and the War Cabinet, of which you were a leading member. I am not prepared to take any more of it lying down. Perhaps you will now be good enough either to justify the allegations, or to inform me that you were misreported and will now disown them."

Attlee's reply was apologetic, accepting responsibility for the bombing policy, and claimed a failing memory. The book was amended, but the statement in the Times was never corrected, as Harris required. He had wanted this out of respect for those lost in the operations and the feelings of their surviving relatives, and in the interest of historical accuracy. In a subsequent letter Attlee accused Harris of being hypersensitive on this subject. Here their correspondence ended. Harris himself, in a brief letter published in the Sunday Times on 22nd January 1961, simply made it clear where responsibility had lain for the wartime decisions about the full bombing policy.

In those raids a total of 55,000 crewmen of Bomber Command had perished, yet at the time they knew it was the only way to stop the Nazi domination and to free the rest of Europe from their oppression.

In 1946 a Dutchman wrote a letter to Marshal of the Royal Air Force Sir Arthur Harris, as he was by then, to thank him for all they had done. It really shows how Bomber Command's efforts helped so many who had suffered the inhumanity of the Nazi regime in those occupied countries of Holland, France, Belgium, Denmark, Norway and our own Channel Islands.

The letter was dated 14th February 1946:

"We shall never forget the nights your squadrons passed over us in the dark on their way to Germany. The mighty noise was like music for us, about happier days to come. Your passing planes kept us believing in the coming victory, no matter what we had to endure. We have suffered much, but Britain and the RAF did not disappoint us and we thank you and the British Nation for our living in peace again."

RAF Bomber Command existed in total for thirty-two years – from 14th July 1936 until 30th April 1968. On that date Bomber Command merged with Fighter Command to become Strike Command. Further land was acquired, a new office block was built for the administrative HQ of the new Command, other buildings were enlarged and modernised and the whole site was then re-designated Royal Air Force High Wycombe. Later, Transport and Coastal Commands joined in the amalgamation of operations to form a single multi-role organisation. Strike Command then operated alongside two other RAF Commands, Personnel and Training Command and Logistics Command.

STRIKE COMMAND

In 1978, a new underground bunker was commissioned to control the operations of Strike Command within the North Atlantic Treaty Organisation (NATO), where computerised advanced radar systems and communications had made the existing installation obsolete.

A twelve-acre site was selected on Hollybush Farm on the edge of the eleven hundred-acre Bradenham Estate, which had been given to the National Trust by Ernest Cook in 1956. This land bordered the existing RAF Headquarters, and was bounded on two sides by existing installations. Handing over of this piece of land within the Green Belt, forming part of the Chilterns Area of Outstanding Natural Beauty, by an organisation dedicated to the preservation of Britain's national heritage, caused uproar. It was also said that it broke a covenant under which Mr. Cook had given the land to the National Trust.

The first indications of this proposal came in reports in the local press. Naturally members of the National Trust were up in arms – it appeared that the negotiations had been completed behind their backs. One of the protesters, Professor George Hutchinson of Southampton University, stated that the Trust had acted in a patriarchal and arrogant fashion.

In its defence, the Trust informed its members that the effects of the Communications Centre had been discussed at length with the local planning authority, the Countryside Commission, the Nature Conservancy Council, the Parish Council and other bodies. Their Regional and Head Office Committees and staff had also subjected it to thorough examination. It was further explained that the land required had no special features. It was used as flat grazing land, situated on a plateau, surrounded by trees and not overlooked from any vantage point. On two sides, the security fence and aerials of RAF High Wycombe already bordered it. There were no public footpaths crossing the land and it would be disingenuous to claim there would be damage to the beauty of the surroundings once the period of construction and landscaping was completed.

The Trust further assured its membership that even before considering the details they had pressed the Ministry hard on the question of alternative sites. They had received categorical assurance that no other suitable site for this purpose exists, neither could it be accommodated within the boundary of the present RAF Headquarters.

Taking all this into account the Trust decided just before the end of the year (1981) that it would be better to grant a conditional lease, rather than resist the application and run the risk of a public inquiry. If the Trust had taken this course, as advocated by some of its critics, it would certainly have lost. It could not argue that the scheme posed a lasting threat to the area. By granting a lease it could obtain some advantages for the estate. A lease gave the Trust far greater control than if it had been lost through a Compulsory Purchase Order.

Although a protest was organised, led by a local Trust member who obtained a three thousand-signature petition, it was too late. A ninety-nine year lease was signed between the Trust and the Ministry of Defence in April 1982 and contractors moved onto the site the following month. In finally resolving this issue the National Trust and English Heritage were able to insist that the bunker would be grassed over and an existing hedge restored, a condition the Ministry of Defence were happy to comply with anyway, as it would aid its own camouflage.

The new four-storey bunker, officially titled the N.A.T.O. Underground Permanent War Headquarters, was eighty metres by thirty metres by twenty-five metres deep. It comprised separate departments for intelligence co-ordination, processing of early-warning information and computerised operations rooms for wartime protection, reconnaissance and strike missions control. Dormitories and canteens were provided to serve the six hundred staff should the underground block need to be sealed off. As well as serving as the main Command Centre in any future war involving Britain, it was also capable of directing air operations for N.A.T.O. from northern Norway to southern Germany and far out into the Atlantic.

With the ending of the "Cold War" period, the budget of the three services came under intense scrutiny and in early 1994 it was announced that a new joint tri-service operational headquarters was to be set up, the most likely choice being the Naval Centre at Northwood, Middlesex. Then in July, a new Strike Command office block was constructed adjacent to the underground operations bunker. This was commandeered by N.A.T.O. as a Principal Subordinate Command HQ for the Air Defence of North-West Europe (AIRNW).

WYCOMBE ABBEY: H.Q. UNITED STATES ARMY AIR FORCE (U.S.A.A.F.)

EIGHTH BOMBER COMMAND

Wycombe Abbey, reconstructed in the eighteenth century by the first Lord Carrington, was sold to a syndicate wishing to establish a girls' school on this prestigious site. At that time Lord Carrington still retained Daws Hill House further up the hill, along with the surrounding four hundred acres of parkland. The school was opened on 23rd September 1896, coinciding with "Victoria Day", the date on which Queen Victoria became our longest reigning monarch.

In 1928, Daws Hill House and the two hundred acres of land were put up for sale as building land. Not wishing to be surrounded by this type of development, the school purchased the land for the princely sum of seventy-five thousand pounds.

The outbreak of war in 1939 had little effect on the school, other than that some of the girls were withdrawn. Nevertheless, with reduced income, it continued under its resourceful headmistress, Miss W. M. Crosthwaite (who had been responsible for the purchase of Daws Hill in the first few months of her appointment). In March 1942, it became known that the school premises and grounds had been inspected with a view to being requisitioned for the expansion of Bomber Command headquarters. On 28th March, the Air Ministry took over the entire property despite vigorous protestations from Miss Crosthwaite.

PINETREE

With the impending arrival of heavy bomber units of the USAAF in the United Kingdom during 1942, a suitable headquarters was urgently required and it was considered prudent to site this close to the existing RAF Bomber Command H.Q. This prompted the hasty acquisition of Wycombe Abbey and the school grounds, the first American officers arriving there on 15th April to set up the headquarters for the USAAF, Eighth Bomber Command. The new headquarters was code-named "PINETREE".

The school itself was to be used for administrative offices for the Eighth's Commanders, Brigadier General (later Lieutenant General) Ira C. Eaker, Lieutenant General James H. Doolittle (from January 1944) and Major General William A. Kepner (from May 1945).

Soon clusters of buildings were erected in the grounds. The western slopes of Daws Hill became a tent city to cope with the accommodation of the H.Q. personnel, which by the war's end numbered some twelve thousand personnel. In little more than eleven months, at a cost of nearly £200,000, an underground bunker was built on the crest of the hill. Initially occupied by RAF Bomber Command it was then shared with the U.S. Eighth Bomber Command, until the Americans finally took over completely.

The 'Pinetree' Command Centre comprised three floors extending over twenty-three thousand square feet, all underground, with a covering of ten feet of concrete and twenty-five feet of soil. The side walls were over six feet thick and were surrounded by a void varying from two feet six inches to four feet, to create a 'a building within a building' to absorb the shock of explosions. Internal walls were five feet thick. The whole was protected with gas-tight doors, air filtration and air conditioning, to maintain an internal temperature of sixty-seven degrees Fahrenheit. The emergency power and water supplies allowed the underground complex to be self-supporting for a considerable period.

Wycombe Abbey School for those three years became the headquarters of the U.S. Eighth Army Air Force, the nerve centre of some of the mightiest daylight air assaults which, in co-operation with the RAF night raids, paved the way to an Allied victory in Europe. Within those walls

were conceived and directed the operations of the world's mightiest strategic air force – 200,000 men and women, 2,400 four-engined heavy bombers and 1,200 fighter aircraft.

At the start, the staff of Wycombe Abbey School had been asked to execute a mass evacuation that would have made the ablest military commander ponder the possibility of its success, given the number of people and amount of equipment and belongings that had to be relocated. Yet the impossible was done in a way that characterised activities in any way connected with the Abbey from its foundation.

A few of the original Abbey staff remained on the premises, including Miss Crosthwaite, as the American forces rolled in, their trucks churning up the once peaceful Abbey grounds. Nissen huts, machine guns, jeeps leapfrogging over the open spaces, giant holes being dug, feverish activities, replaced the quiet of previously untouched fields and hills. Daily, the new residents could be seen wending their way between the Abbey and the camp site at the top of the hill (Camp Lynn, named in memory of the first American airman to go missing in action over Europe, Lieutenant William Lynn). In a very short time it developed into a small city to include parade grounds, baseball pitches, more Nissen huts and tents, a movie theatre, a Red Cross Club, mess halls and kitchens, guard posts and motor pools.

The Abbey lawns on which the girls had played cricket soon began to show the scars of the more vigorous American game of baseball. Inside the Abbey, floors that had been crossed by the light-footed young girls now resounded with the tread of heavy military boots. Rooms that once heard recitations in Latin and Greek echoed to the sound of booming American accents, frantically shouting about matters of keeping aircraft in the air.

The Abbey hall was divided into many separate offices, each with desk and phone – all became hives of activity. At its peak the telephone exchange was handling as many as 14,000 calls a day.

What had been the named Halls of Residence became offices for various purposes. The Public Relations Officer moved into Airlie House, the Engineering Officer into Campbell House, while the Camp Surgeon moved into Barry House. Daws Hill House became the home of the Combined Operations Planning Committee, staffed by officers from the U.S. Eighth Army Air Force and the Royal Air Force. The Intelligence Section occupied part of this building and part of the massive underground Operations Room, which also housed the huge map rooms, Communications Centre and the Operational Planning Section. The buildings of the Photo-reconnaissance Wing Headquarters were situated at the bottom of the hill, to the east of the school. The 7th Photographic Group squadrons were operating from Mount Farm only a few miles away in Oxfordshire.

As the American force continued to build up they decided to take on the task of daylight bombing raids on Germany, to complement the RAF's night raids. At first they faced terrible losses, having mistakenly believed the B17 Flying Fortress was capable of protecting itself against any enemy fighter aircraft. It was only with the arrival of the long range North American P51 Mustang, with its performance transformed when fitted with the Rolls Royce Merlin engine, that this threat was countered.

A light-hearted moment was provided when the famous and well remembered Major

Glenn Miller and his band arrived at Wycombe Abbey on the 29th July 1944, to provide some much needed entertainment. Sadly it was only five months later that he too would be lost in yet another wartime tragedy. Having departed from Twinwood, an airfield near Bedford, on the 15th December 1944, he failed to arrive at his destination, Paris. Reported as missing, the aircraft was never seen again. Most of his band members had arrived in Paris a week previously as preparations were to be made for a show at "Olympia". The band continued playing and supporting the troops with Jerry Gray then conducting, until their final performance on 17th November 1945.

Towards the end of 1944 the Eighth

THE AMERICAN FORCES CLAIMED THAT THEIR PROUDEST MOMENT WAS WHEN THE KING AND QUEEN VISITED THEM AT WYCOMBE ABBEY ON 11th MAY 1945. THIS PICTURE WAS TAKEN AS THEY WERE SHOWN ROUND THE BASE.
IN FRONT, THE QUEEN WITH COLONEL JOHNSON, BASE COMMANDER, NEXT KING GEORGE VI WITH MAJOR GENERAL WILLIAM E. KEPNER, COMMANDING VIII FIGHTER COMMAND. BEHIND IS MAJOR MARY DIXON, COMMANDING THE WACS DETACHMENT.

reached the peak of its operating power. On 24th December, conducted from the Abbey, an armada of 2,034 heavy bomber and 936 fighter aircraft left from airfields in East Anglia to attack the marshalling yards, communication centres and airfields behind enemy lines. This counter-offensive was needed when a German attack on the forward line of Allied troops broke through and retook much of the ground gained during the past months. (Known then as the Battle of the Bulge, it temporarily put the Allies in a desperate situation.)

Today this force is still remembered as the "Mighty Eighth". Over 21,000 American airmen flew on that mission, and many times that number worked on the ground to prepare and guide these aircraft. During 1944 they dropped 43,000 tons of bombs, its crews amassed 1,700,000 operational flying hours and its aircraft consumed 522,000,000 gallons of petrol. More than 3,000,000 bombs and 53,000,000 rounds of ammunition had been expended during this period. They also paid a terrible price for their brave insistence on continuing with their daylight raids. Churchill had very strong misgivings over the higher casualties the Americans were suffering in their determination to keep up a round-the-clock offensive, trying to break the German morale.

Though their heavy bomber aircraft were bristling with machine guns, the loss rate was often higher than 10%. The British heavy bombers, by operating mainly at night, towards the end of the conflict when they had gained control of the skies above Germany, often returned with less than a 2% loss rate.

Claimed by the American forces to be one of their proudest days at the Abbey was 11th May 1945, three days after the German surrender, when the King and Queen paid their visit to the site. The Base Commander, Lieutenant General James H. Doolittle, and his staff took them on a tour of the operations rooms and various other offices. Later the King invested the Lieutenant General with the KCB.

As the early months of 1945 passed, the strategic air assault on Germany came to an end. Their work was completed, yet for two thirds of the Eighth, they still had one more score to settle: Japan. So those veterans of the European war travelled on, not home, but into another theatre of war in the Far East. Often in this country it was known as "the forgotten war". The conflict continued there against the Japanese. Though peace returned to Europe on 8th May 1945, it was another three months before the Japanese were forced to surrender. The new American weapon

the atom bomb had shown them their fate too was sealed.

By January 1945, already with an air of confidence as to the outcome of the war, the school governors at the Abbey were pressing the authorities for an assurance that the school would be de-requisitioned within three months of the ending of hostilities. The headmistress had already received applications for the September term, but receiving an unsatisfactory reply from the Ministry of Education, an approach was made directly to the Air Ministry, which brought the ominous news that they might be considering the permanent acquisition of the premises.

The Chairman of the Governors in reply asked for an assurance that "the buildings would be returned as soon as they were no longer required for the purpose for which they had been requisitioned". In May, the Member of Parliament for High Wycombe, Sir Alfred Knox, raised the matter in the House of Commons. Although Sir Archibald Sinclair, the Secretary of State for Air, gave assurance "that the school buildings will be released as soon as the Allied unit now occupying them had been moved", it was obvious that the reopening of the school would be delayed (until 1946).

In October 1945, it was reported that the remaining Americans, except for some at the camp at the top of the hill, would be leaving by the 25th, but the RAF would then be taking over. The Air Ministry stated that the buildings would be returned when satisfactory agreement on dilapidations had been reached.

By February 1946, there was general agreement between the parties, except that the hand-over would not include the so-called "Protected Area" which included what was euphemistically described as the "Underground Telephone Exchange". When the school governing body met in the following June, the first item on the agenda was a letter from the Air Ministry, concerning the underground accommodation. At the time, the Daws Hill camp with its operations bunker on the top of the hill was still an integral part of the school grounds. The Governors agreed that while they were prepared to grant a lease on this property, they would not agree to the outright sale of any part.

Meanwhile another problem had arisen: the surface buildings of the camp had been taken over by homeless civilians, evacuated from the blitzed areas of London, who eyed the recently abandoned American quarters very favourably and families were soon converting the huts into living accommodation.

Understandably, Miss Crosthwaite was very concerned at this invasion and said she would not re-open for the September term unless a fence was erected between the camp and the school grounds. The town clerk was informed that the Governors were taking every possible step to have the camp vacated, although it was anticipated that this must put the school on a collision course with the local authority who were duty bound to provide housing for the homeless. As expected, the Town Clerk responded with a request to the Governors asking if they would grant the council a lease of the land presently occupied by the squatters. This problem was not resolved until the local housing situation improved and council housing became available in the vicinity.

Arguments still continued regarding the level of compensation payable to the school, with the Air Ministry refusing outright to pay for the removal of the wartime roads in the grounds, the matter not being resolved until May 1949. In December 1950 the Air Ministry offered £125 per annum for a lease of twenty-one years on the underground area, whereupon they would erect a sight-proof fence between the school and the camp. This had been prompted by the desire of the U.S. Strategic Air Command (S.A.C.) to re-occupy the wartime command centre for its United Kingdom-based 7th Air Division. In May 1952, S.A.C. established the 3929th Air Base Squadron there and on 10th September High Wycombe Air Station was officially reactivated as "USAF Site, Wycombe Abbey", as a satellite of the 3911th Air Base Group at West Drayton.

In 1953, the Air Ministry required additional land to expand the camp on Daws Hill and a new lease was agreed with the school in February 1954 for 28 years at £1,600 per annum. This was in anticipation of the move of the 7th Air Division headquarters from its Middlesex base at South Ruislip to High Wycombe. The move made sense, as it would position the headquarters mid-way between the S.A.C. bases in East Anglia and those in the Oxford area and also would be close to the RAF Bomber Command Headquarters. Then, in June that year, a further proposal was received from the Air Ministry, this time to purchase the site outright.

Negotiations opened between the school and the USAF in July but dragged on for over two years before a sale price was finally agreed and contracts exchanged in August 1956. The Air Ministry was to pay £40,000 for the main part of what was generally referred to as the Daws Hill site: to accept a lease for the area of the underground installation for a twenty-eight year period at a nominal £1 per annum (and for an extended period of twenty-eight years at £100 per annum), and give a written assurance that there

would be no tunnelling or boring beyond the area of the leased land.

By 1959, after the 7th Air Division quit four of its East Anglian bases, S.A.C. operations were concentrated in Oxfordshire and High Wycombe was the obvious choice for a central headquarters and, on 1st July 1959, the 3929th Air Base Squadron assumed direct support of the base, the move from South Ruislip being completed by October that year. Over seventy new buildings were constructed and numerous other modifications made, including the addition of extra dormitories in 1960/61.

For the next five years, the station served as the Strategic Air Command's United Kingdom nerve centre during a period of the cold war when S.A.C. and Bomber Command were practically one air force in concept and operation. However, by 1965, with the capability of air-to-air refuelling, the US decided it could provide a higher level of defence direct from bases in the United States.

In June that year, the 7th Air Division at High Wycombe was de-activated as the last step in its withdrawal from the United Kingdom and the base was transferred to the United States 3rd Air Force and the United States Air Forces in Europe. The 7563rd Air Base Squadron then took up residence and provided support for the Department of Defense activities in the London area until the base closed in January 1971. By then, the underground Operations Centre was no longer in use.

In April 1984, the host organisation was re-designated the 7520th Air Base Squadron, coming under the direct control of the 3rd Air Force headquarters at RAF Mildenhall in July 1987, before being finally de-activated in May 1993, the tenure then being handed over to the Commander of United States Navy Activities, United Kingdom. (At the time of writing it is anticipated that the base will be vacated in July 2007.)

THE STORY OF AN AMERICAN GENERAL

Reproduced from the Dec.-Jan. 2006 *"Target"* Magazine, Journal of the Bourne End (Buckinghamshire) Community Association. Copyright John Lunnon, photographs by permission of Alun Hughes and Bill Free.

HIS RIVERSIDE HEADQUARTERS AND HIS FRIENDS.

Those of us locals who were here during the Second World War will remember that the Japanese attack on Pearl Harbour on 7th December 1941 brought the Americans into the war. With little delay, the might of the American war machine started to descend on these islands to join the allied effort to destroy the forces of the Axis Powers.

The Government immediately requisitioned Wycombe Abbey. This resulted in the school's pupils having to move elsewhere for the duration of the hostilities. Such was the rapidity of their exit that the girl's dormitories were taken over intact. Imagine a newly arrived airman studying an old notice pinned to the wall, which read; "Anyone distressed during the night, call for a mistress." Soon earth-moving equipment was busy digging out vast quantities of soil in the construction of underground bunkers at Daws Hill in High Wycombe which became the Headquarters of the United States Eighth Army Air Force.

At the same time the Mill House was commandeered and the then owner, Bernard Frost, and his family were made to vacate at short notice and were re-housed in The Lodge, facing Hedsor Corner. Thus, this lovely Thames-side mansion, with its own swimming pool at the mouth of the River Wye (previously owned by Sir Edward Mountain, Chairman of Eagle Star Insurance) was taken over. When two American military policemen (known as "Snowdrops" with their white helmets) were seen permanently guarding the gates on the corner, before the Ferry Lane turning, news soon got around that they were guarding the personal headquarters of an American General.

History relates that on the 23rd February 1942, Brigadier General Ira C. Eaker was appointed Commander of the US Eighth Army Air Force. On the very same day, 23rd February, Air Marshal Arthur Harris was appointed Commander in Chief, Bomber Command at Walters Ash, just four miles north of High Wycombe.

It so happened that in 1941, as leader of an RAF delegation to Washington to discuss air strategy, he had met General Eaker and established good relations with him. In their new posts an enormous spirit of co-operation continued between the two, which extended to all levels of command. The setting up of an organisation, in which ultimately the US Eighth Army Air Force flew from some sixty-seven airfields in the UK, gives some idea of the degree of co-operation. In January 1944, with preparations for the forthcoming invasion of Europe, a change of command in all theatres of war took place. General Eaker was posted to succeed Air Marshal Tedder, as Chief of Mediterranean Air Command. Tedder was recalled to England to become Deputy to General Eisenhower, appointed as Supreme Allied Commander for the European invasion. On the 31st January 1944 General James Doolittle became Commander of the US Eighth Army Air Force.

It was following a question from the current owner of the Mill House, this year, some sixty years after the war, that I was asked if I might know anything about General Doolittle's stay there. This caused me to make some enquiries. As luck would have it, I heard that General Doolittle's personal driver, Corporal Stan Haynes of the RAF, had revisited the Mill House in 1984 on his eightieth birthday with his son Alan. The then owner, Mr. and Mrs Bill Freeman, were given some wartime photographs from that period which had been Crown Copyright.

U.S. MILITARY POLICE (SNOWDROPS AS THEY WERE KNOWN ON ACCOUNT OF THEIR WHITE HELMETS) ON GUARD OUTSIDE THE GATES OF THE MILL HOUSE, HEDSOR.

Although Stan Haynes is no longer living, I was able to trace his son who lives in Suffolk and have his permission to reprint some of these valuable photographs and record some of the anecdotes he left behind. Also I have been able to renew contact with my dear friend Mary Plaisted, Bernard Frost's daughter, who, having been discharged from the WAAF due to ill health early in 1944, returned to the Mill House Cottage and remembers the General well.

By all accounts General Doolittle was a kindly man and assumed command of the Eighth Army Air Force with a remarkable aviation history. In 1932 he had won the world speed record for land based planes, averaging 204 mph, and won the Thompson Trophy in the Cleveland Air Race. On 21st April 1942 he led sixteen B 25 Mitchell bombers, which had taken off from the US carrier Hornet and made the first American bombing raid on Tokyo, landing on airfields in China. In November that year, as Brigadier General, he commanded the Allied Air Forces in North Africa.

L to R GENERAL JAMES DOOLITTLE, GENERAL IRA EAKER AND
HIS WIFE RUTH WITH AIR MARSHAL 'BOMBER' HARRIS.

This photograph of General James Doolittle, General Ira Eaker with his wife Ruth and Bomber Harris in the foreground with a Cadillac outside the Mill House, may have been historic.

Was it the occasion of General Eaker's first introduction of Air Marshal Harris to General Doolittle in 1944 when he had just assumed command? The shot of the two "Snowdrops" standing to attention outside the Mill House gates will be remembered as somewhat unusual. They were frequently seen lounging in a relaxed position against the Mill House wall. Rumour has it that General Doolittle, after a visit to Bomber Command at Walters Ash, was heard to say, "Why can't you guys stand to attention like the RAF sentries?"

Occasionally a light aircraft, possibly a Piper L4 Grasshopper or a Cessna Bobcat, would land across the river on Cockmarsh. This was the General's son, who was also a pilot in the USAAF.

Father was heard to berate his son, who found difficulty in handling a rowing boat to cross the river, "Having learned to fly how is it you can't handle a simple boat?" According to the General's driver he also had a most considerate and kindly personality. Corporal Haynes had been seconded from the RAF to chauffeur him. Having discovered his wife was still working in London making parachutes, Doolittle saw to it that a job on the domestic staff at the Mill House was found for her and a house in Bourne End, where they could enjoy married life together. Apparently among the staff was a Chinese houseboy called Yikki who was adept at scavenging the well-stocked kitchen garden to produce oriental salads.

According to Mary Plaisted (then Frost), the Mill House, judging by the number of cars coming and going, also housed a sizeable number of headquarters staff, including visits by General Omar Bradley (Commander of U.S. landings on D-Day) and U.S. General Spaatz, (Commander Strategic Air Forces). There was also a continuous round of entertainment, with visits by film stars such as Clarke Gable and numerous starlets as well! In a recent television documentary about Glenn Miller, General Doolittle is shown addressing a crowd of US airmen outside Wycombe Abbey in the summer of 1944, saying words to the effect; "Your music played here today is worth to the morale of my troops, more than a thousand letters from home."

By the end of the war the Eighth had suffered about half the US Army Air Force's casualties (47,483 out of 115,332). In 1944 Doolittle was promoted to Lieutenant General and was created a KCB by King George VI.

Hedsor House was used from 1952 as the United States Secret Telecommunications Headquarters. This was at the height of the Cold War. It continued to be protected by armed members of the U.S. Military Police.

THE TERRACE AND GARDENS OF HUGHENDEN MANOR TODAY.

HUGHENDEN MANOR

*A top secret wartime intelligence establishment
code-named –
"HILLSIDE"*

In what was once the sleepy countryside community of Hughenden, one and a half miles north of High Wycombe, there could be no more idyllic setting than that of Hughenden Manor, resting as it does at the top of the rising land of Hughenden Park. Remote maybe, definitely secluded and quiet, surrounded by many mature trees, beautifully laid lawns and well tended gardens. The view south, forward from the terrace follows the valley towards High Wycombe. In the distance the tower of the parish church can be seen as it rises above the skyline. It is now owned and cared for by the National Trust.

The Manor had been the country home of the great Victorian statesman, Benjamin Disraeli. He became Prime Minister, initially in 1868 when aged 63 and again from 1874 until 1880. In his second term of office his Government was responsible for much social legislation. This included in 1875, the Climbing Boys Act, the prohibition of employing juvenile chimney sweeps, the Artisans Dwelling Act, allowing local authorities to clear slums and provide housing for the poor, and the Public Health Act of 1875, providing sanitation such as running water and refuse disposal. As a Conservative politician, Disraeli achieved lasting fame having initiated a wide range of legislation to improve education and the life of working people. In 1879 he was created Earl of Beaconsfield. On several occasions Queen Victoria visited him at the Manor. He was active until one month before his death from bronchitis in 1881, at Curzon Street, London.

Disraeli's niece, Mrs. Calverley, sold the house in 1937 to W. H. Abbey, who vested it, the remaining contents and 189 acres in the Disraelian Society, so that it could be preserved for the nation.

With the outbreak of the Second World War, like so many other similar properties, it was requisitioned by 'The Military', eventually to be returned to the Disraelian Society in 1946. In 1947, sufficient money was raised to allow the Manor to be gifted to the National Trust, yet the history of its wartime activities remained unknown to the general public. There had been local rumours, tales of something vaguely to do with photography, or maps, some connection with the RAF photographic unit at Medmenham.

Yet it all started to come to light when Mrs. Quaife, the widow of Major Quaife who had been the Commanding Officer at the Manor from 1942 until 1945, visited the manor and was able to hand over papers that had been held by her husband concerning those years. Since 1980 a story has slowly grown about those times, an occasional visitor would mention their part in those activities, often they were requested to leave their names and contact details. Perhaps the most significant of these was when a National Trust volunteer happened to overhear a visitor telling a young lad at his side how he had been there during the war. The young lad was the grandson of this visitor, Victor Gregory. It transpired that Victor had spent the war years working at the Manor as an RAF cartographic draughtsman. Through this chance connection, others who had been involved were contacted, culminating in a reunion held at the Manor on 10th January 2007, where National Trust volunteers were able to make recordings and take notes from these important sources of information. At last the true story of this episode, after all these years, was revealed.

At the start of the Second World War, in 1939, Hughenden Manor had taken up a totally new role when the Air Ministry requisitioned it. It became a top-secret intelligence and map-making facility, from then on identified by the rather appropriate codename – "HILLSIDE". From being a quiet country manor house it changed into a more sinister fortified secret intelligence base.

Armed Air Ministry Police were responsible for security and patrolled the grounds both day and night. At night outside the boundaries of the Manor the Volunteer Defence Force, or Home Guard as they later became, set up a post to observe the approaches to the Manor, challenging anyone that came near.

MAJOR QUAIFE, COMMANDING OFFICER OF HILLSIDE.
PHOTO – National Trust.

When initially requisitioned by the Ministry, the staff at Hillside, under Major Quaife, consisted of a small number of Royal Engineer Surveyors and Cartographers along with some Air Ministry Police and civilians. This was soon to change, as the Royal Engineers were replaced with RAF and WAAF personnel who had been selected and trained for this very specialised work. Major Quaife, a man of great experience in this type of work, remained as the Commanding Officer of Hillside for the entire period of the war. A Mr. Dawson was in charge of Air Ministry Administration.

As RAF personnel started to take over, a photographic unit set up their equipment in the old icehouse and a small RAF Transport Section took up residence in the stable yard. All the printing equipment was installed in the basement, always a very noisy environment. Eventually about one hundred people worked here and most were billeted in the town. Cycles were the means of transport and they would cycle to the Manor in the morning and return to their lodgings in the evening, often a journey of three or four miles each way. Some found they were living in dwellings that had no bathroom. Many of the terraced houses in Wycombe's back streets had a tin bath hanging on the wall outside which was brought inside on Friday night for use by the whole family; this included the new arrivals! Luckily there was a bathroom in the basement of the Manor, which many of them gladly made use of.

The work undertaken would be part of a combined effort including the photo-reconnaissance (P.R.) squadrons at RAF Benson and the photo-interpretation unit at RAF Medmenham, whose aim was to provide the latest intelligence on enemy activity. Eventually there were five P.R. squadrons established at Benson, two with Mosquitos, two with Spitfires and one with a variety of other aircraft. Most were specially-equipped aircraft. Fast, unarmed and capable of flying at great height to avoid being intercepted by enemy aircraft, they would over-fly enemy territory and return with aerial photographs of sites of interest. The personnel at Medmenham, where the films were processed, were then able carefully to study every detail. Models of target zones were often constructed at Medmenham to assist bomber crews to identify target areas for the more important raids.

At the time a new and ingenious technique in aerial interpretation was developed. By taking two pictures of a site at slightly differing angles and super-imposing them, they gave a three-dimensional effect when viewed through special glasses. This proved very successful in this type of intelligence work.

The importance of every detail was highlighted when a young WAAF Flight Officer, Constance Babington-Smith, whilst studying the latest pictures, noticed something unusual. She found what appeared to be a small aircraft on a concrete ramp with scorch marks at the rear.

She had located the new Flying Bomb (V1) research and development site at Peenemunde.

Intelligence reports had already given some indication of a new 'revenge weapon' about to be released on the British population. The threat from such weapons required immediate action. On 17th August 1943 Bomber Command launched almost six hundred bombers in a raid against the site at Peenemunde and destroyed many of the

Government to restrict their distribution. As new maps were produced, many sensitive military, transport and communication sites in Germany were left blank: a deliberate ploy to withhold information from those who might seek to oppose the Nazi cause. Their preparation for taking control of Europe by force had been progressing for several years before our intervention in September 1939.

EXPERT MAP-MAKERS AT WORK IN A DRAWING OFFICE AT THE MANOR.

PHOTO – National Trust

assembly shops and laboratories. At first the raid was considered a great success but eventually it was proved to be of only limited value as the Germans were already building other sites. The force of the raid on Peenemunde influenced the Germans to move their research work deep inside the Harz Mountains, a site impossible to bomb, so the threat continued. Testing was moved to Poland.

Though the continued RAF bombing of new launch sites certainly delayed this project, nevertheless the first V1 flying bomb attacks started on 13th June 1944. Over ten thousand arrived, causing great damage and loss of life. London became like the 1940 blitz over again.

Hillside used the intelligence information gained for producing the most up-to-date maps for future use. Apparently prior to 1939 maps of Germany had been very difficult to obtain. There had been a deliberate attempt by the German

At Hillside the nerve centre was the library. The maps they managed to obtain of Germany were stored here, including many "local maps" of their cities and towns. These proved invaluable in helping to pinpoint important targets. The aim of their dedicated work, using a process of photo interpretation from information gathered by the P.R. missions, was to fill in many of those blank spaces and update the maps with the latest information. Maybe the blank areas were more helpful than hindrance to those studying the maps, making obvious the position of something the Germans preferred to conceal.

When Air Marshal Harris had arrived at the Command H.Q. at Walters Ash (Naphill) in February 1942, as the new Air Officer Commanding-in-Chief (A.O.C.-in-C.) of Bomber Command, work at Hillside became totally focused. He came with a clearly defined role, to increase the aerial attacks on targets in Germany in any way possible, considered the only way effectively to strike back against Nazi tyranny. Maps would be needed that only Hillside could provide. They had to be made and delivered in the short time between the decision to attack a certain target and the attack being made. Though targets were identified maybe weeks before, this information was never passed on in the interest of absolute secrecy – even bomber crews were not informed of their destination until the pre-operation briefing. This secrecy also applied to those who had to supply the maps: they too, were not told until absolutely necessary. The pressure to produce the maps could then be intense.

That year new navigational aids such as "Gee" and "Oboe" were coming into service. At first Gee was considered unreliable. "Oboe", an improved form of "Gee", followed. Both had a limited range. Even so, those early months had begun to show the growing effect of Bomber Command. Raids of two or three hundred aircraft on smaller targets gave encouraging results with "low" loss rates. On the night of 30/31st May 1942, only three months after Harris had taken command, Operation Millennium, the first one thousand bomber raid on Cologne, hit the enemy hard. Their defences were overwhelmed, with the consequence that British losses that night were considered light.

Maps were made for all major bombing raids on the Ruhr, on German cities, the breaching of the Dams, a story in its own right. For the invasion of Europe (D-Day), maps of the whole of the North French Coast along the English Channel were accurately produced at Hillside. The RAF draughtsmen and cartographers became very skilled in their work, putting the whole operation at the leading edge of aerial surveillance. As the months passed, aerial navigation, aided with these maps, also advanced greatly. A Pathfinder Force, formed using only the best navigators and equipment in the command, marked targets with flares and incendiary bombs for the following bomber formations. This improved, beyond expectations, the results achieved. A map created for an attack on the Eagle's Nest (Hitler's retreat in the Bavarian Alps) in April 1945 shows the target clearly defined. (See maps at the end of this section.) When it was carried out, though Hitler was not there, it made it very clear that his time had run out. A few days later (30th April) he committed suicide. On 7th May 1945 Germany surrendered.

The people at Hillside were never allowed to divulge the nature of their work; today's evidence seems to indicate that very little was ever really known about it. Even the wife and daughter of the Commanding Officer, Major Quaife, were unable to tell people where they had been on the occasions they visited him at the Manor. When interviewed about these visits by the National Trust the daughter explained, "On the walls were posters warning 'Careless talk costs lives', or 'Walls have ears'." She became convinced that there were spies behind every wall. Despite all this, it was discovered that Hillside was mentioned at the top of a hit list found in the possession of a German pilot. We shall never know how they found out.

Were any attempts ever made to bomb the Manor? On the 9th July 1944 a V1 Flying Bomb struck Downley, injuring three people and damaging thirteen houses. A second V1 also hit the Hughenden Valley at Four Ashes on the 7th August 1944; the blast from this blew out the "Te Deum" window, commemorating Disraeli, in Hughenden Church. The third V1 struck Gomme's sports field at Totteridge. All were within a two mile radius of the Manor.

These weapons, though never considered accurate, had a devastating blast which did great damage when they hit a built up area. Their short range necessitated launch sites to be placed along the north coast of France. These were soon overrun after the invasion of Europe on the 6th June 1944.

In 1946 the Air Ministry moved quietly out of the Manor, their work completed. In 1947 the Abbey family and the Disraelian Society made over the Manor and its grounds to the National Trust, and the work to return it to the country home as Disraeli had known it began.

During their occupation, the Air Ministry had removed and stored all furnishings: walls and floors were left bare. The National Trust very carefully restored it all. For many years now, through their efforts, the public has been able to enjoy the history of this building. Learning of its early times, of the Prime Minister Benjamin Disraeli and his efforts to improve the lot of the working class, now we can know the full story of those dark war years, when we all depended on the diligence of those who held the secrets of "Hillside". It must be said, at first all were reluctant to tell their stories. Only after the Trust received permission from the Ministry of Defence did they willingly reveal all.

Today, while taking one of the pre-arranged guided tours at the Manor, we are fortunate to be able to listen to the recorded wartime experiences of some of the people who worked there during those war years.

Chapter 6

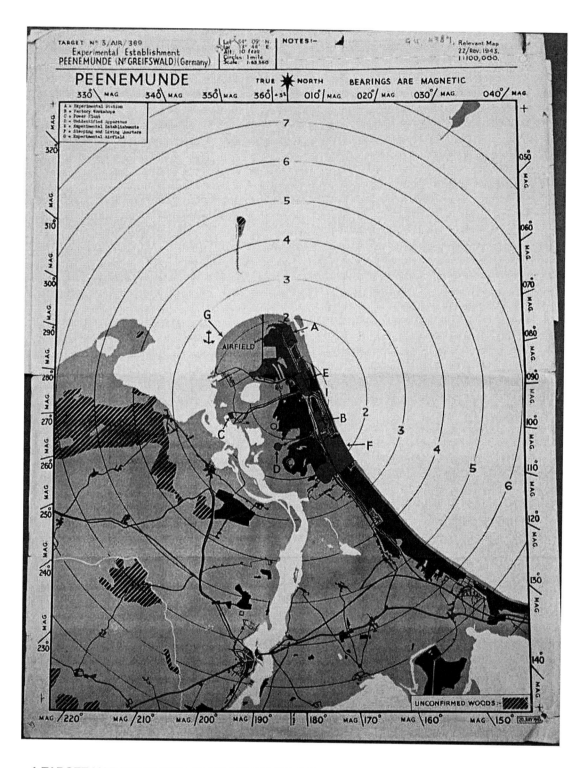

A TARGET MAP PRODUCED AT 'HILLSIDE' FOR THE RAID AGAINST THE V1 (FLYING BOMB) ROCKET RESEARCH SITE AT PEENEMUNDE ON 17th AUGUST 1943. OF THE 596 AIRCRAFT THAT TOOK PART IN THE ATTACK, 41 NEVER RETURNED.

Map – Air Ministry.
Source Hughenden Manor.

95

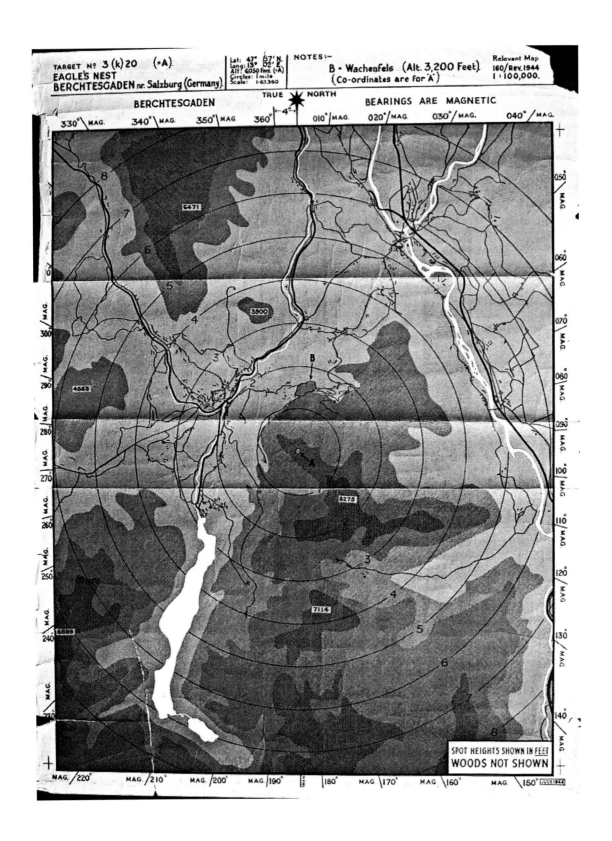

IN APRIL 1945 A BOMBING RAID WAS MADE TO DESTROY HITLER'S BAVARIAN
MOUNTAIN RETREAT AT BERCHTESGADEN, KNOWN AS THE EAGLE'S NEST. THOUGH IT
WAS SUCCESSFULLY CARRIED OUT, HITLER WAS NOT THERE.

Map - Air Ministry.
Source Hughenden Manor.

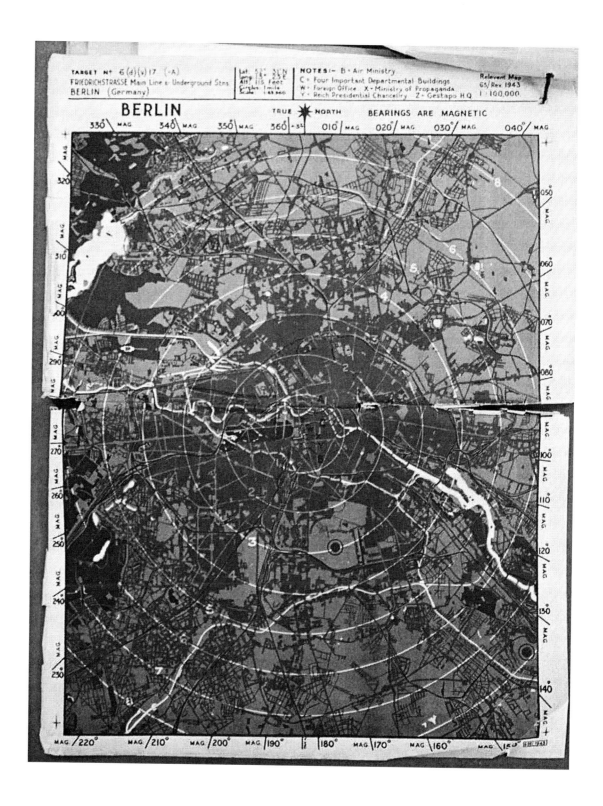

THIS DETAILED MAP OF BERLIN CLEARLY MARKS THE TARGET. ALSO NOTE THE ROUND BLACK DOT IN A BLACK CIRCLE. IT IS IN THE MIDDLE OF ONE OF THOSE AREAS LEFT BLANK ON GERMAN MAPS PRINTED IN THE 1930s.

Map - Air Ministry.
Source Hughenden Manor.

Liste Zielsatz L

Zielgruppe 13

Kasernen, Kommandostellen, Schulen

Spalte 1 Ziel Nr.	Spalte 2 Bezeichnung des Zieles	Spalte 3 K. Bl. Nr. 1 : 100 000	Archivunterlagen St.K.	a	bc	b	c	Spalte 9 Bemerk.
13 1	High Wycombe, Schloß Hughenden, Stabsqu. d. Fighter Command.	E 29	O	O			O	
13 2	Harrogate, 1. Hotel Majestic, 2. Hotel Esplanade, Stabsqu. d. Luftfahrtministeriums	E 9	O	O			O	
13 3	Stanmore, Stabsqu. d. Bomber Command.	E 29	O	O	O			Z.K. 1 b
13 4	Ruislip, Rec. Off. d. R.A.F.	E 29	O	O	O			Z.K. 1 b
13 5	Portsmouth, Kasernen	E 38	O	O	O			Z.K. 3/4
13 6	Canterbury, Kasernen	E 40	O	O	O			
13 7	Swindon-Watchfield, Kasernenanlage	E 28	O	O	O			
13 8	Portsmouth-Hilsea, Kasernen	E 38	O	O	O	O		Z.K. 3/4
13 9	Pembroke Dock, Kasernenanlage	E 20	O	O	O			Z.K. 8 a
13 10	Prestatyn, Kasernenanlage	E 11	O	O	O	O		
13 11	London, Whitehall, Kriegsministerium	E 34		O		O		Z.K. 1 b
13 12	London, Mayfair Square, Admiralität	E 34		O		O		Z.K. 1 b
13 13	London, Mayfair Square, Neues Luftfahrt-ministerium, Techn. Amt	E 29/34		O		O		Z.K. 1 b
13 14	London, Thames House, Zentrbür. d. Flugzeugprod.	E 34		O		O		Z.K. 1 b
13 15	London, Savoy Hotel u. Somersethouse Zentralbüro d. Flugzeugproduktion	E 29/34		O		O		Z.K. 1 b
13 16	London, Somersethouse u. Tothill Street, Versorgungsministerium	E 91/34		O		O		Z.K. 1 b
13 17	London, Tothill Street, Inform.-Ministerium	E 34		O		O		Z.K. 1 b
13 18								
13 19								
13 20								
13 21								
13 22								
13 23								
13 24								
13 25								
13 26								
13 27								
13 28								
13 29								
13 30								

Zgr. 13, Bl. 1

CAPTURED GERMAN TARGET LIST

THIS TARGET LIST 13 (ZIELGRUPPE 13) WAS FOUND CONCEALED IN THE BOOT OF A GERMAN PILOT. AT THE TOP OF THE LIST IS SCHLOSS HUGHENDEN. The nearest interpretation for this word Schloss in this context is Castle. How had they found out that it was something worth targeting?

National Trust

CHAPTER 7

WYCOMBE AIR PARK

(BOOKER AERODROME)

"Wycombe Air Park", better known to older locals as "Booker Aerodrome", is located three miles south west of High Wycombe, within the Parish of Great Marlow. Originally the Wycombe Borough boundary ran along the northern edge of this area. The history as far as can be ascertained today shows the Manor, of which Wycombe Air Park only forms a small part, had been given to the Hospital of St. Thomas of Southwark with an endowment from the Clare family. More recent information shows the Morris family owned and farmed this land from 1890 until 1937, when it was known as Barmoor Farm. It was sold in 1938, after the death of Tom Morris, to a Mr. Wetton, who hoped to set up a flying school there. The Morris family continued to live in the farmhouse for some time after the aerodrome opened.

The planning application shows it was originally conceived as a civil aerodrome and it was hoped to enlarge the site to enable the granting of an all purpose licence. (See meeting minutes, May 1939 Item 4:1.) Claims that it was originally named "Marlow Airport" appear to be incorrect, as no official evidence of this has been found. As will be noted throughout the planning application it is referred to as "Proposed Aerodrome, Booker". The only change to this was on the 1st June 1941, when it was taken over by the RAF as a Military Airfield. (The description as "Airfield" was adopted to follow American practice.)

The dated information following (minutes from the planning meetings) shows the progress made for the proposed aerodrome. As would be expected it did have its objectors.

24th April 1939

PLANNING APPLICATION

Application submitted by Mr. W. H. Wetton, for approval to use Barmoor Farm, Great Marlow, as a Civil Aerodrome. The land has an area of 256 acres and is bounded by Clay Lane, Booker on the east side, the Marlow-Stokenchurch Road on the south side and the boundary of Wycombe Borough on the north side.

The Planning Committee understand that the Civil Aviation Department of the Air Ministry have inspected the site and are prepared to grant a

licence, subject to the satisfactory laying out of the ground.

It was reported that there are three dwellings on the east side of Clay Lane immediately opposite the site and three houses on the west side of Horns Lane adjoining the site. The Isolation Hospital is sited 300 yards east of the boundary of the site and beyond this distance development is rather comprehensive, adjoining Booker Common and Cressex Lane. Land to the south and east is mostly of an agricultural nature.

The Clerk read a letter from the Wycombe Joint Hospital Committee requesting the Committee to refuse the application on the grounds of the injurious effect on the Isolation Hospital.

Letters were also received from Brig. M. R. Wootten, the West Wycombe Estate and the Penn Branch of The Council for the Preservation of Rural England, asking that the application should be refused.

A petition was submitted, signed by 75 residents in the vicinity of the site and asking the Committee to reject the proposal.

After consideration of the application it was proposed by Mr. G. C. Tew, seconded by Mrs. Oakeshott, that the application be refused on the grounds of the proximity of the Isolation Hospital. On being put forward to the Meeting, four members voted for the motion and five against. It was therefore decided to notify the Joint Town Planning Committee that the Committee were favourably to consider recommending to the Council the granting of the necessary Interim Certificate, the matter be further considered before the Council on the 1st proximo, after a further recommendation had been received from the Joint Town Planning Committee.

1st May 1939

Meeting of the Interim Development (Town Planning) and Plans Committee of the Wycombe Rural District Council.

Present:- Mr. W. H. Wootten (Chairman); Mrs. C. Oakeshott; Mrs. E. M. Porri: Mrs. E. .F. Quicke; Brig. Gen. E. S. Hoare-Nairn; Capt. B. W. Richards; Mr. G. T. Cantle Beaumont; Mr. W. G.

Britnell; Mr. G. C. Tew; Mr. J. Pearce; Mr. W. Pitch, Mr. T. E. Collier.

1. PROPOSED AERODROME, BOOKER

The Clerk reported upon the recommendation by the Joint Town Planning Committee, that this application be approved, subject to the following conditions:-

That the aerodrome shall not be laid out otherwise than to the satisfaction of the Council and the runways so arranged that the amenities of existing properties to the east shall be safeguarded as far as possible.

That no hangars or ancillary buildings shall be erected unless their design, materials and location shall have previously been approved by the Council.

That no industries shall be established on the site without consent of the Council.

That the promoters shall use their best endeavours to obtain additional land required to enable an all-purpose licence to be granted.

That the promoters indemnify the responsible authorities against any claims for compensation which might arise, either as a result of the restrictions on the height of the buildings adjoining the aerodrome which it would be necessary to prescribe in the Planning Scheme or otherwise.

That the trees adjoining the west side of Horns Lane and Clay Lane, known as Hazel Grove, shall be retained and indicated as protected woodlands in the Scheme subject to reasonable vehicular and flying access.

That in the event of the aerodrome ceasing to be used as such for a period exceeding six months, that the promoters or the other owners for the time being of the site, shall forthwith clear the site of all erections, stores and materials and so far as is possible, restore the land to its state at the granting of the interim certificate.

2. NEW BUILDING BYLAWS

The Committee considered the New Building Byelaws and it was proposed by Mr. W. G. Britnell, seconded by Mr. J. Pearce and RESOLVED that the Minister of Health be requested to give his approval thereto.

22nd May 1939

PROPOSED AERODROME, BOOKER

The Clerk reported on the correspondence in regard to this proposal and that he would be having an interview with Mr. W. H. Wetton in regard to the conditions under which the Committee's approval was given.

5th June 1939

PROPOSED AERODROME, BOOKER

A layout of the undermentioned buildings was submitted for consideration: -

Two Bellman Hangars, each 170 feet long by 90 feet wide. One Semi-Permanent Hangar, 350 feet long by 200 feet wide. Workshops and Stores. Administration, Mess and Crew Rooms. Details for the last mentioned to be submitted later.

All the buildings, with the exception of the Administration Block, are situated on the north side of the existing farm road and immediately adjoining Hazel Grove, which forms a screen between the proposed buildings and Clay Lane. A few trees are proposed to be felled to straighten out the boundary, but a uniform belt of trees, 260 feet wide, is proposed to be retained. The administration block is immediately to the south of the farm road.

Resolved that the layout be approved, subject to the approval of details by the Clerk and Planning Officer.

26th June 1939

PROPOSED AERODROME, BOOKER

Together with Mr R. H. Herring, the Planning Officer had interviewed Mr. Wetton and Mr. Wetton had undertaken that no engine tuning would be carried out in the workshops and also that the running up of machines, tuning and other mechanical adjustments, which create noise, would be carried out as near the north-east corner of the site as practicable.

Plans were submitted for the semi-permanent hangar in an approved position. The building is to be 350 feet long by 200 feet wide and covered with corrugated asbestos, with patent glazing in the roof.

Resolved to approve the proposal and request Mr. Wetton to use green coloured asbestos sheets for the building.

One purpose envisaged for the new aerodrome would be the setting up of a school for training RAF Volunteer Reservists. The company name proposed by Mr. W. H. Wetton was Wetton Aviation and it began operating as No. 50 Elementary & Reserve Flying Training School (ERFTS), with RAF Tiger Moth, Hawker Audax and Hawker Hind aircraft. Some years prior to this the RAF Director of Training had decided that elementary flying training of pupil pilots would be carried out at civilian schools. This was to leave the RAF flying training schools to continue with advanced training, relieving pressure on front line units.

ORIGINALLY A PRIVATE VENTURE, THE START OF THE NEW AIRFIELD AT BOOKER IN 1939. SHORTLY AFTER OPENING IT WAS TAKEN OVER BY THE RAF.

Photo BFP.

At the outbreak of war though, in common with all civilian operated flying schools, Wetton Aviation School was closed down. It was then acquired in 1939 by the Air Ministry from its owner, Mr. (later Wing Commander) Wetton. Airwork General Trading Company bid for the training contracts and was successful in winning a contract for RAF ground servicing and flying training, which included Booker Aerodrome. Shortly after, the technical site was constructed on the eastern boundary of the landing area and this contained four Bellman Hangars. Some hutted accommodation was located adjacent to the technical side and the remainder sited on the opposite side of the minor road, which formed the eastern boundary. The grass runway lengths (in yards) during the Second World War were - N/S 970, NE/SW 1133, E/W 920 and SE/NW 900.

As a military airfield, Booker was commissioned for use on 1st June 1941 and occupied by No 21 Elementary Flying Training School (21 EFTS), 50 Group, Flying Training Command. The unit was classified as a "Type A Operated Unit", supported by the civilian contractor Airwork Ltd. Night flying training commenced on 21st October 1941 with the aid of a "Cranwell Type" flare path and a Relief Landing

Ground (RLG) was established at Bray, where flying commenced on 5th July 1941. Bray, however, proved to be unsuitable, therefore an alternative RLG was established at Denham on 31st October 1941. This acted as the main RLG for Booker throughout the war, closing on 9th July 1945. It was planned to operate four flights at Booker and two at Denham.

Flying training commenced on 5th July 1941, with an initial intake of one hundred and twenty RAF student pilots. (Some sixty of these were from No 13 EFTS at Peterborough, which was closed down.) The first aircraft to be operated were Tiger Moths, of which seventy-two were allocated to Booker in 1941, thirty-two were flown by instructional staff and the remainder by the Air Transport Auxiliary. Courses ran for seven weeks with an average of fifty-five flying hours per month. In addition to Tiger Moths, the unit eventually operated Miles Magisters, Airspeed Oxfords, Austers, North American Harvards and Percival Proctors.

Although the first courses were aimed at RAF students, with ab-initio pilot training and pilot grading prior to training overseas, the unit quickly became involved with the training of Army personnel, with the first group of ten officers enrolled for Course No. 26 on 1st October 1941.

In 1942, however, the main focus of training shifted to initial training for glider pilots, using the Tiger Moth. The No. 1 Glider Course commenced on 13th May 1942, with forty-five troops of No. 1 Company of the 1st Glider Pilot Regiment. The course was to be of twelve weeks duration and new courses were scheduled to commence every three weeks. The instructors were very happy with this new course, as it helped them to improve their flying skills and gave them back a personal interest in their students' progress, both of which had been slowly disappearing as a result of the Pilot Grading Courses. In addition to UK students, eleven Turkish Officers were attached for flying in April 1942.

The No. 1 Course graduated on 29th July 1941. Of the original forty-five students, four Officers and thirty-one NCOs passed, two Officers were transferred to No. 3 Course, two NCOs failed examinations, four were suspended due to lack of flying ability and one was suspended on disciplinary grounds. The remaining student was the first Army student to lose his life at Booker. Sgt. A. Terry's Miles Magister (T 1889) caught fire on landing at Taplow and he was killed instantly.

Some of the instructors at Booker, all of whom would have been operational pilots prior to becoming instructors, wished to return to operational flying themselves. Eventually on 4th August 1942, their wish was granted when they were given the opportunity to apply for conversion training to undertake further operational tours.

It was policy to rest pilots who had finished a tour of duty (consisting of a specified number of operational flights). Many of them were posted to flying training schools as instructors, passing on their experience to those new entries. Some, though, still sought the thrill of battle and could not wait to get back to operational flying.

Though Wycombe was generally very fortunate in avoiding air raids, on 29th August 1942, the war came to Booker in the form of a damaged Handley Page Hampden returning from a bombing raid. The aircraft (AT 143) overshot the airfield attempting a forced landing, ploughed through a hedge on the southern boundary and stopped on the road. Fortunately there were no casualties, but the aircraft was badly damaged. A few weeks later, on 26th September, a Spitfire from the Photographic Reconnaissance Unit at Benson force-landed under similar circumstances.

nerve and abandoned the aircraft. He was suspended from flying training."

Another incident involved a student "being struck by a rotating propeller". It was reported that he "sustained serious injuries, but the aircraft was undamaged."

On the 18th May 1943, H.R.H. Prince Bernhard of the Netherlands visited 21 EFTS. Other notable visitors to Booker, some of whom may have learnt to fly there, included: King Zog of Albania; Clark Gable (who was living in Bourne End); James Stewart; Theodore Roosevelt; Cecil Lewis (Flight Commander "A" Flight and former WW1 flying ace); and Dudley Steynor, RAFVR, (who later became a gliding instructor at Wycombe Air Park, only retiring in 1994 at the age of 84). The recorded number of hours flown by 21 EFTS in July 1943 was 5,576 of which 442 were at night.

On the 23rd August 1943, a Miles Magister, carrying an unauthorised female passenger, crashed. Sadly both pilot and passenger were killed.

A ROW OF DH 82A TIGER MOTHS ON THE FLIGHT LINE

Photo. LEWIS PERRIN

Although there was a great deal of flying training taking place at Booker, the number of accidents was relatively low. On 1st March 1943, a Tiger Moth (N6557) crashed into a wood near Gerrards Cross. Although the aircraft was destroyed, the pilot parachuted to safety. On further investigation, however, it was found that "It appeared that the pilot allowed the aircraft to get into a stalled condition at 3,000 feet, lost his

In October 1944, RAF glider courses commenced training RAF SNCOs as glider pilots. These courses ran alongside the Army courses already under way and were supplemented by refresher courses for operational pilots returning from flying duties. The success rate for all courses at Booker was extremely high and the unit was regularly commended on its performance, with an

AN AIRSPEED OXFORD BETWEEN THE HANGARS AT BOOKER.

Photo. JOHN BEECHEY

average pass rate for all courses reported to be 80%. Many of the pilots trained at Booker progressed to operational tours and many of the glider pilots distinguished themselves during the D-Day landings and at the Battle of Arnhem.

In Salisbury Cathedral there is a Roll of Honour to those glider pilots who were trained at Booker and later killed in action. It amounted to one third of those brave pilots, who had no form of defence once in the air. On landing the glider they were to leave immediately, to endeavour to return to their unit by any means possible.

This unit was probably the longest-lived EFTS, not being disbanded until 28th February 1950. Following the war, 21 EFTS continued pilot training for both powered and glider pilots and in 1947 training was again extended to include Royal Navy students.

The disbanding of 21 EFTS did not signal the end of RAF Booker, as No.1 Basic Flying Training School (1 BFTS) was formed here in February 1951. This unit with 20 Chipmunk T.10 aircraft, again supported by Airwork Ltd., commenced training RAF Cadet Pilots on 7th February. A number went on to serve in the Korean War.

The Public Records Office at Kew has a bound volume of several hundred pages, containing records and photographs of No.21 EFTS.

NEAREST THE CAMERA IS AN AIRSPEED OXFORD, USED FOR CREW TRAINING AND COMMUNICATIONS WORK. ALONGSIDE IS A GRUMMAN AVENGER.

Photo. LEWIS PERRIN

To enhance operations at the airfield, a PSP (Pierced Steel Planking) runway and taxi track was installed in August 1951. This was 07/25, 900 by 30 (yards) wide, outlined in white. The other grass runways (all in yards) were:– NE/SW 1200, N/S 1100, NW/SE 800 and E/W 870. Also a VDF Homer, Eureka, Approach and Tower Radio on 130.86 were added, but there was no fixed lighting. The airfield identity was indicated as "BV".

DH CHIPMUNK BEING CHECKED OUT BEFORE FLIGHT.
Photo LEWIS PERRIN

The locals nicknamed the training aircraft the "Booker Bombers" and there are tales of low flying antics, with reports of low flying along Marlow High Street and turning at the end to avoid the church spire.

The Commanding Officer from 1941-46 was Wing Commander O'Donnell.

SOME NOTEWORTHY EVENTS, WHILST BOOKER REMAINED AN RAF AIRFIELD:–

A P38 Lockheed Lightning (probably from Mount Farm, Oxfordshire) landed with photographs for the Photographic Interpretation Centre at Medmenham.

Australians and New Zealanders were stationed here in 1945/6.

5th November 1947, 21 EFTS took over responsibility for the training of Army Glider and Air Observation Post Pilots.

No. 126 Gliding School operated at Booker from August 1943 to September 1955.

Joint Services Staff College Flight, operated by Airwork, from Booker, from January 1947 to November 1952.

July 3rd 1954, Manchester University Air Squadron arrived and stayed until 31st July, equipped with 13 Chipmunks and 1 Harvard. Personnel included 11 Officers, 29 Cadet Pilots and 3 Airmen.

July 4th 1954, Liverpool University Air Squadron arrived with 12 Chipmunks and 1 Harvard. They had 8 Officers, 25 Cadet Pilots and 1 Airman.

From October 1950 to January 1956, London University Air Squadron operated Chipmunks.

No. 1 BFTS was eventually disbanded on 20th July 1953.

From October 1946 to March 1963, Bomber Command Communications Flight operated various aircraft types including Percival Pembroke, DH Devon, DH Chipmunk and Avro Anson aircraft. This Flight was temporarily relocated to RAF Halton and RAF Benson while the single hard runway (06/24, 804 yards long) was laid in 1958.

A Cessna 310 of the USAF was stationed here and there were occasional visits by USAF Dakotas.

In 1962 the airfield was downgraded to "Care and Maintenance," and the Communications Flight moved to RAF Bovingdon and became the Metropolitan Communications Unit.

Wycombe Air Park (Booker Aerodrome) as a Civilian Airfield.

1963-64. No flying took place and the airfield was used for flying model aeroplanes.

1965. The airfield was taken over by 20th Century Fox and used to represent Brooklands Aerodrome during the early years of aviation and for the filming of *"Those Magnificent Men in their Flying Machines"*.

Later in 1965, The Airways Aero Association (BEA/BOAC Flying Club) relocated to Booker from White Waltham and re-named it "Wycombe Air Park." Prior to White Waltham they had been at Croydon, Biggin Hill and Denham.

The Silver Wing Gliding Club (restricted to BEA and BOAC personnel) started a Gliding Association.

Wycombe Air Centre was started by Tony Gyselynck in 1967, initially operating with Rollason Condors, later changing to Cessna 150s and 172s. This organisation is still operating but was taken over by Cabair in 2006.

In 1968 Doug Bianchi moved his company, Personal Plane Services (P.P.S.), here from White Waltham. They specialised in aircraft maintenance, restoration and provision of services to the Film Industry. These activities continue at Wycombe Air Park to this day, now run by his son, Tony Bianchi.

Their involvement in Film and Television work has included many notable epics:- *Those Magnificent Men in their Flying Machines, Aces*

High, Rollerball, The Avengers, James Bond and Some Mothers do 'ave em (Michael Crawford).

P.S. Engineering work is concentrated mainly on restoring historic aeroplanes and amongst these temporary residents are included Spitfires, Tempest, Mosquito, Lysander, Dragon Rapide, Cierva Autogiro and Dakota, to name but a few. At the time of writing, a Spitfire Mk. 1a is undergoing a complete restoration. A Curtis Travel Air 2000 (formerly used in film work to represent a Fokker D.VII) is being rebuilt to flying condition, with parts of the repairs/rebuilding of the wooden airframe structure being undertaken by Ian Simmons (co-author of this book).

The "Blue Max Film Aviation Museum" was here for some years, open to paying members of the public, before being relocated to Compton Abbas airfield in Dorset. A replica Sopwith Camel and Fokker Eindekker, both based at Compton Abbas, along with other aircraft, are still kept available for film work. Tiger Moths and Stampes have, in the past been "modified" for film work, to represent aeroplanes from a much earlier era.

In 1983, the airfield operation was taken over by the Airways Aero Association, with the main activities operated by British Airways Flying Club, Wycombe Air Centre and Booker Gliding Club. Airways Aero Association have a forty-year lease from Wycombe District Council, which runs until 2015.

Inside the main entrance to the airfield a Memorial Stone has been erected (incorporating a carving of a Tiger Moth propeller) to all those RAF and Army personnel who had served at RAF Booker from 1941 – 1955. It was unveiled on the

11th September 1999. The ceremony was organised by Wycombe District Council with the dedication carried out by Reverend Dyfen Wynne-Jones (padre of RAF High Wycombe) and unveiled by Lieutenant Colonel Nick Nicholls of the Glider Pilot Regimental Association.

ON THE BASE ARE THESE WORDS –

"IN MEMORY OF THE PILOTS WHO TRAINED AND SERVED AT R A F BOOKER 1041 1945, ESPECIALLY THOSE WHO GAVE THEIR LIVES IN THE SERVICE OF THEIR COUNTRY"

Photo I.C.S.

AT THE CORONATION OF QUEEN ELIZABETH II, THESE CHIPMUNKS WERE ASSEMBLED AT BOOKER AIRFIELD AND WOULD LEAD THE CORONATION FLYPAST OVER LONDON.

Photo. ROGER SMITH

AN UNFORTUNATE OVERSHOOT, THIS AVRO ANSON ENDED UP ON THE LANE END ROAD.
MID 1950s. NO CASUALTIES.

Photo . RONALD GOODEARL

AT THE TIME OF WRITING THE
OCCUPANTS OF BOOKER AIRFIELD
INCLUDE :-

British Airways Flying Club,

Cabair (formerly Wycombe Air Centre),

Booker Gliding Centre,

Helicopter Services Ltd.

Personal Plane Services (PPS),

Parkhouse Aviation.

Approximately one hundred and twenty aircraft are
resident at the airfield.

There is one asphalt runway (06/24 753 metres x
23 metres) and two grass runways (06/24 610 x 23
and 17/35 695 x 30)

Air Traffic Control operates on 126.55 MHz
(tower) and 121.755 MHz (ground) frequencies.

Three of the original four hangars have now been
replaced by Reid Steel type.

<u>Appendix 1</u>

Participants in the de Havilland Commemorative Fly-past on 27/7/2000, flying over the birthplace of Sir Geoffrey de Havilland (originally Magdala House but now renamed Terriers Green House), at Terriers Green, Nr. Hazlemere, High Wycombe.

<u>A magnificent flypast of fifteen pre-war de Havilland aeroplanes.</u>

Those participating were: -

DH 80A Puss Moth.	Tim Williams.	G-AAZP.
DH 82A Tiger Moths.	Peter Henley.	G-ACDJ.
	Mark Blois-Brooke.	G-ANEH.
	Alistair Davy.	G-ANEL.
	Liz Gliddon.	G-ANOH.
	Colin Dodds.	G-AXBW.
	Keith Pogmore.	G-AZZZ.
DH 84 Dragon.	J. J. Sullivan.	EI-ABI "Iolar".
DH 85 Leopard Moths.	Carolyn Grace.	G-ACMN.
	Desmond Penrose.	G-ACUS.
DH 87B Hornet Moths.	Adrian Davy.	G-ADKC.
	Terry Holloway.	G-AHBL.
	Paul Gliddon.	G-AHBM.
DH 90 Dragonfly.	Henry Labouchere.	G-AEDU.
DH 94 Moth Minor.	John Davy.	G-AFPN.

All these aircraft are over sixty years old and in most cases cared for by their owners, yet what a wonderful tribute they are to their designer Geoffrey de Havilland and all the craftsmen involved with building them.

APPENDIX 2. Bucks Free Press, Situations Vacant columns1917/18.

A selection of the adverts with their dates that appeared in the Bucks Free Press:–

Sept. 21ˢᵗ & *Oct. 5ᵗʰ 1917.*	*Aeroplane wood workers (skilled) wanted at once. Cabinet-makers suitable. Good opportunity for good live men. Apply - H. Connelly, 35, Queen's Road, H/W.*
Oct. 5ᵗʰ 1917.	*Machinists wanted for aeroplane work. Apply – Walter Skull & Son Ltd., London Road, H/W.*
Dec. 7ᵗʰ 1917.	*Woodworkers (male) required immediately for aeroplane work. Apply - Walter Skull & Son Ltd., London Road, H/W.*
Dec. 7ᵗʰ 1917.	*Cabinet-makers, Joiners, Wood Craftsmen and Labourers required immediately for aircraft work. Apply – The Davidson Aviation Co., Ltd., Grafton Street, H/W.*
Dec 7ᵗʰ 1917.	*Engineer's fitter required. Apply – The Davidson Aviation Co., Ltd., Grafton Street, H/W.*
Dec. 7ᵗʰ 1917.	*Woodworkers wanted for plane assembling, also spindle moulding machinists. Apply – E. Gomme, Leigh Street, H/W.*
Dec. 14ᵗʰ 1917.	*Woodworkers (male) required immediately for aeroplane work. Apply - Walter Skull & Son Ltd., London Road, H/W.*
Dec. 14ᵗʰ 1917.	*Cabinet-makers, Joiners, Wood Craftsmen and Labourers required immediately for aircraft work. Apply – The Davidson Aviation Co., Ltd., Grafton Street, H/W.*
Dec. 14ᵗʰ 1917.	*Aeroplane work. Machinists wanted also chair-makers, cabinet-makers and improvers. Apply – C. P. Vine, Dashwood Ave., H/W.*
Dec. 14ᵗʰ 1917.	*Aircraft. Wanted – Working Foreman to take charge of aircraft department. Apply - G. H. & S. Keen, Frogmoor, H/W.*
Jan. 4ᵗʰ 1918.	*Chair makers, Cabinet-makers, Benchmen and Machinists wanted for aircraft work. – E. Gomme, Leigh Street, H/W.*
Jan. 4ᵗʰ. 1918.	*Woodworkers (male) required immediately for aeroplane work. Apply - Walter Skull & Son H/W.*
Jan. 4ᵗʰ. 1918.	*Cabinet-makers, Joiners, Wood Craftsmen and Machinists required immediately for aircraft work. Apply – The Davidson Aviation Co., Ltd., Grafton Street, H/W.*
Jan. 4ᵗʰ 1918.	*Wanted. Working foreman for aeroplane work. G. H. & S. Keen Frogmoor H/W.*
Jan. 12ᵗʰ 1918.	*Woodworkers (male) required immediately for aeroplane work. Apply - Walter Skull & Son H/W.*
Jan. 12ᵗʰ 1918.	*First class spindle hands and planers required for aircraft work. Apply – Wm. Bartlett & Son, Sheraton Works, H/W.*
Jan. 12ᵗʰ 1918.	*Cabinet-makers, Joiners, Wood craftsmen and Machinists. Required immediately for aircraft work. Apply – Wm. Bartlett & Son, Sheraton Works, H/W.*
Jan. 12ᵗʰ 1918.	*Wood machinists wanted, also good spindle hand. – Croydon Aviation and Engineering Co. Ltd. 36 Queens Road, H/W.*
Jan. 12ᵗʰ 1918.	*Wanted. Working foreman for aeroplane work. G. H. & S. Keen Frogmoor H/W.*
Jan. 12ᵗʰ 1918.	*Workers wanted for aeroplane work. Apply – F. Parker & Sons, Ltd., Frogmoor Gardens, H/W.*
Jan. 26ᵗʰ 1918.	*Woodworkers (male) required immediately for aeroplane work. Apply - Walter Skull & Son H/W.*
Jan. 26ᵗʰ 1918.	*First class spindle hands and planers required for aircraft work. Apply – Wm. Bartlett & Son, Sheraton Works, H/W.*

Jan. 26th 1918.	*Cabinet-makers, Joiners, Wood craftsmen and Machinists. Required immediately for aircraft work. Apply – Wm. Bartlett & Son, Sheraton Works, H/W.*
Jan. 26th 1918.	*Aeroplane woodworkers wanted. Apply – Thomas Glenister Ltd., H/W.*
Jan. 26th 1918.	*NEW AIRCRAFT FACTORY, High Wycombe. Wanted - Clerk for checking materials and timekeeping. Storekeeper. Typist (male or female). Discharged soldiers given preference. Apply by letter only, stating experience, age and salary required, to The Wildey Company Ltd., Hughenden Ave., H/W.*
Jan. 26th 1918.	*Marker out required to take charge of timber for aviation work. Good wages. Wm. Bartlett & Son, Sheraton works, H/W.*
Jan. 26th 1918.	*Wanted. Working Foreman for aircraft work. Apply - G. H. & S. Keen Frogmoor H/W.*
Jan. 26th 1918.	*Wanted chair makers and cabinet-makers for aircraft work. Apply R. Tyzack, Slater Street, H/W.*
1918.	*Wire worker and splicer required for aircraft work. Apply Wm. Bartlett & Son, Sheraton works, H/W.*
Oct. 18th 1918.	*WYCOMBE AIRCRAFT CONSTRUCTORS Ltd. Managing Director- F. H. Payne. Notice to Woodworkers not engaged in war work. The Company are now prepared to receive applications for employment in their new factory upon its completion. All men not engaged on war work are therefore invited to apply at the High Wycombe Employment Exchange, where forms of application can be filled up.*

Appendix 3. Aircraft crashes and mishaps around High Wycombe.

Extracts from "The Chiltern Prangs" Researched and compiled by Ron.Setter, Peter and Pearl Halliday, of the Chiltern Aircraft Reseach Group.

DATE	AIRCRAFT TYPE	SERIAL NO	UNIT	LOCATION	DETAILS/PILOT
28/07/1911	Birdling Monoplane	not known		Saunderton	Forced landing in Mr.Saunders' meadow due to deteriorating weather. Pilot, Mr. H.J.D.Astley, taking part in the Daily Mail flying competition offering a £10,000 prize to the winner.
14/09/1912	Cody No.5 Cathedral biplane	not known		Downley	Forced landing in cold and windy weather. Also suspected defective compass. Pilot, Samuel Franklin Cody, passenger, his son Leon . Resumed journey, (from Farnborough) to Hardwick Camp nr. Cambridge, Sunday evening.
19/04/1915	Bregeut AG4		2 Sqn.	Little Marlow	Forced landing, no damage. Pilot, Morris Collardean.
??/??/1918	SE 5			Princes Risborough	
??/08/1918	Vickers Virginia	J7438	58 Sqn.	Penn	Crashed, Puttenham Farm. Worthy Down Unit.
??/??/1936	D.H.Dragon			Princes Risborough	
16/07/1936	Gloster Gauntlet	K5264	111 Sqn.	Beaconsfield	Dived into ground, Pilot Gardiner killed.
02/08/1938	Hawker Demon Mk 2	K5903	29 Sqn.	Speen	Hit ground behind Flower Bottom Farm. Nr. Plough Inn. Crew bailed out unhurt. P/O. Brett, LAC Miller.
30/11/1939	Handley Page Hampden	L4203	185 Sqn.	Widmer End	Crashed, Grange Farm, 4 fatalities. Sqn. Ldr. Hope, F/O. Musgrove, Sgt. Thomas, AC2 O'Reegan.
11/12/1939	Handley Page Hampden	P1267	76 sqn.	Princes Risborough	Hit tree in forced landing (poor visibilty). 1 fatality, Pilot C.D.Stevenson.
27/08/1940	Hawker Hurricane Mk1	P3897	1 Sqn.	Bryants Bottom/Speen	Pilot lost control in serchlights and abandoned aircraft.
08/10/1940	Boulton Paul Defiant Mk1	N1627	264 Sqn.	Widmer Farm, Marlow	Crashed due to enemy action, 21.50 hours. 2 fatalities. P/O. H.I. Goodall & Sgt. R.B.Young, commissioned P/O on day of crash..
1941	Spitfire P.R.			Turville Heath	Crashed at Balhams Farm. Polish pilot died.
17/03/1941	Hawker Hurricane Mk1	Z7010	Dely Flt.	Princes Risborough	Crashed at Holy Green. Henlow to Hullavington. 1 fatality. Capt. P.Randel, buried at Maidenhead.
26/03/1941	D.H. Puss Moth,	DP850	Dely Flt.	Beaconsfield	Crashed in forced landing, overturned.
10/07/1941	D.H.Tiger Moth	T6111	21EFTS	Booker	Crash landing.

110

Date	Aircraft	Serial	Unit	Location	Notes
22/07/1941	D.H.Tiger Moth	N6669	21EFTS	Marlow	Controls jammed 2 miles N.E. Marlow.
12/09/1941	D.H.Tiger Moth	T5532	21EFTS	Booker	Stalled on overshoot.
26/09/1941	D.H.Tiger Moth	T5981	21EFTS	Great Missenden	Crashed in forced landing.
08/01/1942	D.H.Tiger Moth	T5363	21EFTS	Saunderton	Hit high tension cable.
10/02/1942	D.H.Tiger Moth	T7111	21EFTS	Booker	Spun into ground.
18/02/1942	D.H.Tiger Moth	R4882	21EFTS	Booker	Stalled on approach.
13/03/1942	D.H.Tiger Moth	T7092	21EFTS	Princes Risborough	Hit high tension cable.
12/04/1942	D.H.Tiger Moth	T6815	21EFTS	Booker	Stalled on overshoot.
13/10/1942	D.H.Tiger Moth	T6444	21EFTS	Princes Risborough	Hit high tension cable, low flying.
25/10/1942	D.H.Tiger Moth	DE456	21EFTS	Booker	Collided with DE619 on approach.
25/10/1942	D.H.Tiger Moth	DE619	21EFTS	Booker	Collided with DE456 on approach.
04/12/1942	D.H.Tiger Moth	T7100	21EFTS	Booker	Spun in on approach.
07/12/1942	Handley Page Halifax Mk 2	DT544	158 Sqn.	Hughenden	Crashed on Green Farm, returning from raid on Mannheim.
30/01/1943	Avro Anson	L1794	Cent. Nav. School	Princes Risborough	Crashed at Longdown Farm. 4 fatalities.
28/03/1943	D.H.Tiger Moth	DE544	21EFTS	Ibstone	Crashed at Manor Farm. 2 fatalities, F/O Harvey, (N. Z.) and P.Gatfield, (ATC), buried at High Wycombe.
29/03/1943	D.H.Tiger Moth	DE176	21EFTS	Booker	Lost control on take off.
10/03/1943	Miles Master Mk 1	V1076	21EFTS	Booker	Swung on take off and hit T9803.
16/05/1943	D.H.Tiger Moth	DE447	21EFTS	Booker	Heavy landing, destroyed by fire.
07/08/1943	Vickers Wellington Mk 1C	R1508	21 OUT	Beaconsfield	Crashed at Browns Wood.
01/10/1943	D.H.Tiger Moth	T6387	21EFTS	Booker	Collided with Magister T9750 on overshoot.
01/10/1943	Miles Magister	T9950	21EFTS	Booker	Crashed after colliding with Tiger Moth T6387.
13/11/1943	B 17G Flying Fortress	23138	306 B.G.	Princes Risborough	Crashed after encountering severe turbulence and icing when forming up for operation. Crew bailed out, pilot killed, (1st Lt C.W. Cosper.) Monument outside Risborough Library.
1944	Dakota			Northend	Blackmoor Wood. 7 fatalities.
14/01/1944	P.38 Lightning		P.R.U.	West Wycombe	Crashed at West Wycombe railway station, 1 fatality, pilot, W. Blickendorfer.
23/02/1944	Messerschmitt Me 410	Not known	KG2 or KG51	Radnage	Crashed at Andridge Farm, Radnage at 12.40am. 2 killed, identity confused, either Lt. F. Miller and Gefr.K.H. Borowski, of Unit KG2 -or- Gustaff Delph and Heinz Ebling of Unit KG51. Aircraft on photo-reconnaissance mission.
16/03/1944	D.H.Tiger Moth	N9157	21EFTS	Booker	Crashed on landing.

Date	Aircraft	Reg.	Unit	Location	Notes
31/03/1944	Handley Page Halifax Mk3	LW579	51 Sqn.	Stokenchurch	Returning from raid on Nurenburg, crashed at Cowlease Wood, 7 fatalities, Pilot P/O. Brooks, Flt.Sgts. D.A. Churchill, S.Glass, D.P. McCormack and G.W.West, Sgts.T.S.Connell and R. Kelly.
11/05/1944	D.H.Tiger Moth	DE244	21EFTS	Booker	Bounced on landing and stalled.
14/06/1944	D.H.Mosquito F.8	N5555	8CC	High Wycombe	Crashed into railway embankment, Pinions. 2 fatalities, pilot - Cpt. W.O.Gurnard and Sgt. E.B. Lynch, (both USAAF). Parts of engine at DH Heritage Museum.
18/07/1944	Handley Page Halifax Mk 3	LK794	578 Sqn	Bisham	Crashed at Applehouse Hill en route for Caen, 6 fatalities, Pilot F/O V.Starkoff, Nav. P/O Fink, Bomb Aimer, Flt. Sgt. Morgan, Wireless Op. P/O Hopper, Flt. Engineer, Sgt Nicholson, Air Gunner Flt. Sgt. Claque. 1 survivor, Flt. Sgt. Sloan.
11/08/1944	D.H.Tiger Mcth	N6674	21EFTS	Booker	Crash landed.
12/08/1944	B 17G Flying Fortress	2107191	398 B.G.	Penn	Crashed on Lude Farm and blew up, 9 fatalities, Pilot, Flt / Lt. C.J.Searl; Co Pilot, A.L.Dion; Bomber, Lt. L.Walsh; Nav. S.Kemper; Sgts. Wilson, Beatty, Bearffel & Kennedy. One crew member, Snyder, suffering severe toothache, not on flight.
26/08/1944	2 Vickers Wellingtons	MF589 HF519	83 OTU.	Prestwood	Mid air collision with Wellington HF519. Following information includes both aircraft. 11 fatalities & 1 survivor,(survivor not known). 1st a/c crew, Pilot, F/O Michielsen & 5 crew. 2nd a/c crew Pilot, F/O E. Smith & 4 crew.
19/09/1944	Airspeed Horsa Mk 1	PF714	1 HGMU	Bourne End	Tug lost power and cast off. Hit pole and truck in forced landing at Well End.
21/10/1944	Dakota			Princes Risborough	Crashed in thick fog at 10.30 AM, Kopp Hill, 6 fatalities.
07/12/1944	Handley Page Halifax Mk 5	LK952	1667 OTU.	High Wycombe	Crashed at Keep Hill and exploded.
02/03/1945	D.H.Tiger Moth	T8262	21EFTS	Lane End	Stalled and dived into ground at Lane End.
19/03/1945	Handley Page Halifax Mk 3	NP939	425 Sqn.	High Wycombe	Belly flopped with engine on fire at Handy Cross. Last aircraft lost by 425 Sqn. In WW2.
05/04/1945	Lancaster Mk 1	RF150	424 Sqn.	Booker	Crashed at Widdington Woods near Booker airfield, returning from raid on Merseburg. On its eigth trip. 7 fatalities. Pilot F/O J.W.Watson; Nav. F/O J.Rockford; Bomb Aimer, Flt. Sgt. C.N.Armstrong; Wireless Op. W/O2 S.Thomson; Flt Eng. Sgt. E.T.Ashdown; Mid Gunner, Flt. Sgt. S.J.Robinson; Rear Gunner, Flt.Sgt.C.J.Howse.
06/04/1945	D.H.Tiger Moth	T7355	21EFTS	Booker	Crash landed.

Appendix 3

Date	Aircraft	Serial	Unit	Location	Description
23/04/1945	D.H.Tiger Moth	T5837	21EFTS	Booker	Crash landed.
29/04/1945	Hawker Hurricane	LF334	41 OTU	Stokenchurch	Engine cut and crash landed.
25/07/1945	D.H.Tiger Moth	DE884	21EFTS	Booker	Overturned on landing.
08/08/1945	D.H.Tiger Moth	T7914	21EFTS	Booker	Crashed on landing.
06/02/1946	D.H.Tiger Moth	NL999	21EFTS	Booker	Undershot landing and hit fence.
12/02/1946	D.H.Tiger Moth	T6196	21EFTS	Little Kimble	Low flying hit high tension cables and crashed at Round Hill Farm, 2 killed.
11/04/1947	D.H.Tiger Moth	NL998	21EFTS	Booker	Undershot landing at night and undercarriage collapsed.
30/09/1948	D.H.Tiger Moth	T5822	21EFTS	Booker	Swung on overshoot and hit a hut.
20/04/1949	D.H.Tiger Moth	DF149	21EFTS	Booker	Hit windsock on approach and overturned.
07/11/1949	D.H.Tiger Moth	R4923	21EFTS	Princes Risborough	Stalled on practice approach and forced landed.
14/02/1950	D.H.Tiger Moth	NM176	21EFTS	Booker	Hit ground on approach.
26/10/1950	Percival Proctor C4	NP196	31 Sqn.	Great Kingshill	Engine cut and crash landed in field.
08/03/1951	Handley Page Halifax C.8	G-AJZY		Great Missenden	Lancashire Aircraft Corporation "Air Monarch", crashed Hyde Lane and burnt out. Inward bound for Bovingdon from Gothenburg. 4 fatalities. Pilot, Cpt. D.Alty; Flt. Officer, J.O.Sullivan; Radio Op, D.A.Issett; Eng. Officer, M.G.Glue.
25/05/1951	D.H.Chipmunk T.10	WB607	London UAS	Booker	Hit high tension cable during practice forced landing.
09/02/1953	Auster AOP 6	VF605	657Sqn.	Great Missenden	Flew into snow cloud, iced up and hit hedge in forced landing in field at Motley Bottom.
20/07/1953	D.H.Chipmunk T.10	WB 705	1BFTS	Booker	Undershot during short landing practice and hit air raid shelter.

SECOND WORLD WAR V1 FLYING BOMB INCIDENTS AROUND HIGH WYCOMBE.

The first 3 V1, (vengence weapons) Flying Bombs, (also known as Doodle Bugs) were launched on the 13th June 1944, one landing in Grove Road, Bow, London, killing 4 people and injuring 32. The other lande at 4:13am in Swanscombe Kent. No record of the third.The attacks soon intensified, mostly being aimed at London, only three are recorded in the Wycombe vicinity

19/06/1944	Flying Bomb V1	High Wycombe	10.35pm. Gommes Sports Field, Totteridge. No Casualties
05/07/1944	Flying Bomb V1	High Wycombe	5.05pm. Downley, 3 Casualties, 13 houses damaged
22/07/1944	Flying Bomb V1	Marlow	6.30pm. Chalk Pit Lane. 2 casulties, Jim Platt then aged 10 (owner of Platts Garage in Marlow) & his Grandmother. House badly damaged.
07/08/1944	Flying Bomb V1	High Wycombe	7.40am. Four Ashes, Hughenden. No Casualties, blast damage to the Disraeli comemorative, (Te Deum) window in Hughenden Church.
??	Flying Bomb V1	Lane End	Mid day Sunday. Hit the Telephone Exchange at Lane End.